Blessing or Curse

Books by Derek Prince

Biography
Appointment in Jerusalem
Derek Prince: A Biography

Guides to the Life of Faith
Atonement: Your Appointment with God
The End of Life's Journey
Faith to Live By
God Is a Matchmaker
God's Remedy for Rejection
The Grace of Yielding
How to Fast Successfully
Husbands and Fathers
The Marriage Covenant
Rediscovering God's Church
Rules of Engagement
Shaping History through Prayer and Fasting
Spiritual Warfare
Thanksgiving, Praise & Worship
They Shall Expel Demons
Through the Psalms with Derek Prince
Transformed for Life
War in Heaven

Systematic Bible Exposition
The Spirit-Filled Believer's Handbook
Promised Land
Self-Study Bible Course

Blessing or Curse

YOU CAN CHOOSE

Third Edition

Derek Prince

Chosen

Grand Rapids, Michigan

© 1990, 2000, 2006 by Derek Prince Ministries–International

Published by Chosen Books
a division of Baker Publishing Group
P.O. Box 6287, Grand Rapids, MI 49516-6287
www.chosenbooks.com

Printed in the United States of America

Library of Congress Cataloging-in-Publication Data
Prince, Derek.
    Blessing or curse : you can choose / Derek Prince.—3rd ed.
        p.   cm.
    Originally published: c1990.
    Includes index.
    ISBN 10: 0-8007-9408-7 (pbk.)
    ISBN 978-0-8007-9408-8 (pbk.)
    1. Success—Religious aspects—Christianity. 2. Blessing and curs-
ing. 3. Blessing and cursing in the Bible. I. Title.
    BV4598.3.P73 2006
    248.4—dc22   2006014241

To protect the privacy of some of the individuals referred to, names of persons and places, and some other details, have in a few cases been changed.

Contents

Foreword

The author of this book was my mentor and spiritual father. It was the privilege of my wife, Bonnie, and me to assist this great servant of God and work alongside Derek Prince as co-pastors for eighteen years. Over the years, we started traveling as an apostolic team. Derek would often have me hold the evangelistic and healing services.

Our lives have been influenced and transformed by the profound truths Derek Prince shared with us. He was our friend and senior elder. He stewarded these truths with grace and integrity, with joy and humor, and without religiosity or legalism.

On our first pilgrimage to Israel, Bonnie and I shared dinner with Derek and Ruth Prince on the shores of the Sea of Galilee. He insisted on buying me St. Peter's fish. As the steaming platter came out, Derek, with a serious face, told me it was customary for pilgrims on their first journey to Galilee to eat the eyes of this fish in honor of St. Peter. Being a good disciple, I immediately bit into them. It was the most terrible stuff I had ever tasted. As I was wiping my tongue with some wet towels, I looked up. Derek was grinning. He loved to tease his friends with practical jokes.

Over the years, I saw for myself the practical outworking of the truths shared in this book in the lives of countless people in Africa, America, Asia and Europe.

I recall our mission trip to Zambia. We were ministering deep in the interior of Africa, overlooking the Zambezi River, where thousands of area villagers had gathered to hear God's Word. Derek, Ruth and I stayed in a nearby ramshackle house with big holes in the roof. Lizards would often drop through the roof as Derek would instruct the lead pastors and share a simple lunch of soup and bread.

A big field had been cleared close to the river, and a large crowd had gathered to hear the truths shared in this book. And we saw wonderful miracles, affirming that many experienced great deliverances from curses that had yoked them for generations. In the late evening, we would walk back through the bush to our lodging, carefully holding kerosene lanterns so as not to step on the abundant poisonous snakes that slithered all around.

As those humble African pastors said farewell, they thanked us and observed, "The last notable ministry team to visit us before yours was Dr. David Livingstone's. Thank you for this message. Now we know we don't have to be afraid of the sorcerers and their curses. The curses can be broken. We have heard and seen that the power of the cross triumphs over all."

In those great apostolic journeys with Derek Prince, I saw the greatness of the Gospel message, the breaking of curses and the importance of the blessing. I saw that these truths can transform and heal families, cities and nations. We are to lay hold of the blessing for ourselves, our children and our nations, as did Jacob in the book of Genesis.

When Rebekah pushed Jacob to the front of the line to receive his father's blessing, she was on a mission from God. Jacob feared discovery, but his mother said, "I'll take the curse. You obey my voice." Rebekah had gone from barren to doubly blessed. Some twenty years after her sons were born, the second of those twins inherited the blessing of a firstborn son. According to tradition, Jacob should not have gotten the blessing. According to his abilities, Jacob should not have gotten the blessing. According to the word of his own father, Jacob should not have gotten the blessing.

But the power of a blessing that comes from God is stronger than any curse the world or man can bring down! The power of the blessing that comes from God will overtake any power of destruction or failure chasing you. The favor that came on Jacob was the blessing of God on His friend Abraham, Jacob's grandfather. The covenant promise that God had made to Abraham was alive and active, even generations after Abraham had died. That covenant and those promises were the root and foreshadow of the promise and blessing that come to you and me through faith in Christ.

The shadow of the cross falling over a person's life is more powerful than any other shadow. Jesus took the curses of sin and death that we might receive the blessings of obedience to His Word. In the cross we are redeemed from every curse. Ultimately poverty, failure, disease, violence, destruction and even death must stop before the shadow of the cross that Jesus raised up for our lives.

The turmoil Rebekah experienced caused her to fear that something terrible was happening. It drove her to God, and she discovered the secret of His blessing. The key to receiving the ongoing blessing was obedience to the voice of God.

Centuries after His promise to Abraham, God delivered some three million of Abraham's descendants from slavery and death in Egypt. How did He do it? He did it by the power of the blood of a lamb. Today, two thousand years after His death and resurrection, the power of the cross of Christ still prevails in breaking curses and releasing the blessing.

Bonnie and I pray that you will be touched and transformed by my friend's great teachings on how to recognize and release yourself from curses. May you and your family always walk in the blessings. It is, as Derek would emphasize, because of the cross.

Mahesh Chavda
senior pastor, All Nations Church
Charlotte, North Carolina

Introduction

In the 1970s Derek Prince began to unfold for believers an astonishing, life-changing teaching from the Bible that few people had ever heard. It was a thoroughly scriptural and God-blessed message about blessings and curses.

This startling revelation—which he would continue to develop and gain spiritual insight about over the next three decades—has profoundly influenced several generations of theologians and preachers. More importantly, it has provided a simple key to a better life for hundreds of thousands of Christians all over the world.

Derek Prince may not be familiar to you. He is not a household name in Christian circles today. Nevertheless, he stands as one of the truly extraordinary Bible teachers and theologians of the twentieth century.

A British citizen born in India, Prince was Eton-educated and Cambridge-trained (a contemporary and acquaintance of C. S. Lewis there). For a time prior to his dramatic conversion experience, he held a prestigious fellowship in ancient and modern philosophy at Cambridge. But once his amazing intellect was submitted to Christ and illuminated by the Holy Spirit, he became a formidable force for communicating the truths of Scripture. As a classically trained philosopher and unabashed charismatic, he was that too-rare confluence of academic rigor and openness to the supernatural. The Word and power. Truth and Spirit.

Across the better part of five decades, in countless cities on six continents, Derek Prince taught, preached, encouraged, proclaimed, imparted and inspired. And all along the way he wrote. It would be difficult to overstate the impact and influence this humble, self-effacing teacher has had around the world.

In the autumn of 2003 Derek Prince died in his beloved Jerusalem—his home for nearly twenty years. He was 88. He left behind some wonderful gifts. To those who had the privilege of knowing him, he left an inspiring example—one of yieldedness to God, love for the Church, a heart for Israel and a roaring passion to see God's people walk in the fullness of the freedom and authority Christ purchased for them.

To all of us he left an astonishing volume of teaching in books, articles, sermons and letters. You now hold in your hands a unique fragment of that treasure. In this newly revised and expanded version of *Blessing or Curse: You Can Choose*, you will find a helpful corresponding study guide at the end of each chapter.

We are confident that as you absorb and apply the truths you will find herein—whether you are studying alone or as a group—you will discover truths to help you walk in greater freedom, blessing and heavenly effectiveness than ever before.

May you truly experience all of the blessing Jesus died to purchase for you.

Introduction to the
Blessing or Curse Study Course

We are delighted to include in this new third edition of
Blessing or Curse: You Can Choose a study course for group
or individual use. These lessons, which appear at the end
of each chapter, include review questions about that chapter (with answers at the end of the study), life application
questions for meditation or discussion, a memory verse
and a faith response.

We have also added testimonies to the beginning of each
of the three sections of the book to encourage you.

Getting Ready

- Pray at the start of each chapter, asking the Holy Spirit
  to teach you.
- Read the chapter.
- Once you have finished, tackle the study. Record your
  answers on a separate sheet of paper. (It is important

that you record your answers; you will use them in later studies.)

- Read the memory verse aloud and later commit it to memory.
- Speak the faith response.
- Pray at the close of each study, asking the Holy Spirit to confirm what you have learned and apply it to your life.

Memory Verse Helps

- It is easiest to memorize a verse one phrase at a time. Read the phrase several times; then try saying it from memory. Do this until you have the phrase memorized. Go to the next phrase and add that to the previous one. Read both together several times; then try saying both phrases from memory. Do this until you have memorized both phrases. Continue with the rest of the verse, phrase by phrase.
- Write the memory verse on a 3 x 5 index card. Carry the card with you or put it in a place where you will see it every day. Say the verse several times a day.
- Use the verse in prayer and meditation.

Section 1

Blessings and Curses

This day I call heaven and earth as witnesses against you that I have set before you life and death, blessings and curses. Now choose life, so that you and your children may live. . . .

Deuteronomy 30:19, NIV

Introduction

It could be you and your family. Or the family next door. Or the person who works with you. Whoever it may be, his or her life is a history of disappointments, frustrations and even tragedies. Somehow the story never ends.

Conversely, we all know families who are similar in background and social position—and yet trouble never seems to touch them. They are almost "too good to be true."

In both cases, invisible forces are at work that determine each person's destiny, whether for better or for worse. The Bible identifies these respectively as *blessings* and *curses*. Furthermore, it shows us how to relate to these forces in such a way that we can enjoy the beneficial effects of the one and protect ourselves from the harmful effects of the other.

A scriptural understanding of both blessings and curses, and how they work, will give you a totally new perspective on your own life, and an answer to problems that have hitherto perplexed and frustrated you.

> This teaching has changed my life. Looking back on the past, I really don't think I'd be alive today if I had not heeded the teachings on self-inflicted and generational curses.
>
> C. B.

1

Wrestling with Shadows

To the superficial observer, human life presents a confused mingling of light and shadow, arranged according to no recognizable pattern, governed by no discernible laws. Across this scene two men may start out walking side by side. Similar in background and ability, they are headed in the same direction. Yet one walks almost always in the light of success and fulfillment. The other, close by him, scarcely sees the light. He is continually overshadowed by failure and frustration, and his life is snuffed out at an untimely age.

Neither of these men understands the forces at work in his life. The sources of light and shadow are hidden to them both. Probably they have never even considered the possibility that both light and shadow may have their source in previous generations.

The Bible speaks plainly about these forces. In fact, it has a great deal to say about them. It calls them respectively *blessings* and *curses*.

Let us look closer, for a moment, at the man under the shadows. He does all the right things: changes his job or place of residence; acquires further vocational skills; studies all the latest literature on positive thinking. Perhaps he even takes a course on how to release some mysterious "potential" within himself.

Yet success eludes him. His children are rebellious, his marriage under strain, accidents and illnesses routine. His cherished goals slip through his fingers like water through the fingers of a drowning man. He is "haunted" by a sense of inevitable failure, which he can perhaps postpone, but never overcome.

All his life he has the sense of struggling against something he cannot identify—something amorphous and elusive. He feels at times as if he is wrestling with a shadow. No matter how hard he struggles, he cannot pinpoint the cause of his problem or get a grip on it. Often he feels like giving up.

"What's the use?" he exclaims. "Nothing ever goes right for me! My father had the same problems. He was a failure, too!"

The person under the shadows could just as well be a woman, of course. She has married young and started out with all sorts of plans for a successful marriage and a happy home. She finds herself, however, on an invisible teeter-totter—"up" one day and "down" the next. Physically, she goes from one problem to another, always on the verge of health, but never quite achieving it. Her son begins to abuse drugs and then her husband leaves her. One day she wakes up to the shocking realization that she herself has become an alcoholic.

Like the man under the shadows, this woman, too, did all the right things. She studied books on nutrition and child psychology. In her pursuit of success, she goaded herself on from one effort to the next—each one demanding all the strength that she could muster. Yet she watched other women, with less motivation or qualifications, achieve the goals she herself could never attain.

As you look closer at the person under the shadows, perhaps you see something that reminds you of yourself. You feel as if you are looking at your own life—but somehow from a point outside yourself. With a shock, you begin to wonder if the cause of your problems could be the same: *a curse going back to preceding generations.*

Or again, it may not be yourself that you see, but someone close to you—a spouse or a family member or a dear friend. You have often agonized over this person and longed for some ray of hope, but always in vain. Now you are confronted with a possible explanation of the shadows, which is a new idea to you. Could the root of the problem really be a curse?

Your mind goes back to events and situations in your life or that of your family that never seemed to make sense. You tried many times to dismiss them from your thoughts, but never completely succeeded. You realize that you need to know more. *Suppose I am the one under a curse,* you may say to yourself. *What can I do? What could be its source?*

A curse could also be likened to a long, evil arm stretched out from the past. It rests upon you with a dark, oppressive force that inhibits the full expression of your personality. You never feel completely free to be yourself. You sense that you have potential within you that is never fully developed. You always expect more of yourself than you are able to achieve.

Or again, that long, evil arm may have the effect of tripping you up as you walk. Your way seems clear before you, but from time to time you stumble—yet you cannot see what it was you stumbled over. For some uncanny reason, the moments at which you stumble are those when you are within reach of attaining some long-sought goal. Yet your goal eludes you.

Actually, the word *uncanny* could be likened to a red warning light. You experience events or situations for which

19

you can find no natural or logical reason. It seems that there is some force at work that is not completely subject to the usual laws of nature or of averages.

There is one word that sums up the effects of a curse: *frustration*. You reach a certain level of achievement in your life and everything looks set for a bright future. You have all the obvious qualifications—and yet something goes wrong! So you start all over again, and reach the same level as before, but once again things go wrong. After this happens several times, you realize it is the pattern of your life. Yet you cannot see any obvious reason for it.

Many people have shared with me the story of a life that has a similar pattern. The individual details may differ, but the pattern is there. Often such people say something like, "The same thing always happened to my father. I feel as if I'm reliving his frustrations," or, "I can hear my grandfather saying again and again, 'Things never go right for me.'"

This pattern may occur in various areas of people's lives: business, career, health or finance. Nearly always it has some kind of negative effect on personal relationships—especially marriage and family. Frequently, too, it affects not just one isolated individual, but a larger social group. Most often this would be a family, but it can extend to a wider circle, such as a community or a nation.

It would be misleading, however, to suggest that a curse always causes a person to fail. A person may achieve what appears to be real success and yet be plagued by frustration, never enjoying the fruits of success.

On a ministry journey in Southeast Asia I met an intelligent, well-educated female judge, who was descended from royalty. She knew Jesus personally as her Savior and was not conscious of any unconfessed sin in her life. Yet she told me that she was not truly satisfied. Her successful career and her high social position had not brought her personal fulfillment.

20

As I talked with her, I discovered that she was descended from many generations of idol worshipers. I explained to her that, according to Exodus 20:3–5, God had pronounced a curse on idol worshipers down to the third and fourth generations. Then I showed her how to receive release from this curse through Jesus her Savior.

Sometimes curses may not have their origin in previous generations. They may be the result of deeds or events in your own lifetime. Or it may be that a curse from previous generations has been compounded by things you yourself have done. Whatever the source of your problem, however, one thing is certain: You are struggling with something that you can neither identify nor understand.

Like that judge, you, too, may have tasted success. You do indeed know the sweetness of it—but it never lasts! Suddenly, for no reason you can explain, you are dissatisfied. Depression settles over you like a cloud. All your achievements seem so insubstantial.

You look at others who appear content in similar circumstances, and you ask yourself, *What's wrong with me? Why don't I ever experience real fulfillment?*

Perhaps at this point your reaction is something like this: *Some of these descriptions really fit me. Does that mean there is no hope for me? Do I have to go on like this for the rest of my life?*

No, there is hope for you! Do not be discouraged. As you read on, you will discover that God has provided a remedy and you will be given simple, practical instructions on how to apply the remedy in your own life.

Meanwhile, you will find encouragement in the following letters I received from two people who listened to my radio Bible-teaching program on the theme "From Curse to Blessing." The first letter is from a man and the second from a woman.

> I listened to your messages on the curse and I found out that I had been under one for years and never knew it. I was

21

never able to be successful in life, and constantly suffered from feelings of homosexuality, though I never fueled the feelings into action. I have been a Christian for 10 years now but because of the curse was never able to get as close to God as I wanted to. I became very depressed.

Since I have been freed from this curse I have felt so free in Jesus and alive in Him. I have never felt so close to God!

·:·

Thank you for your recent broadcasts on curses and your booklet "From Curse to Blessing." My life has been greatly changed by them.

For most of my life I have been troubled by recurring depression, and altogether for five years I have been under the care of a psychiatrist.

This spring a lady prayed with me and for me and I renounced all involvement with the occult, such as tarot cards and tea leaves. Praise the Lord, the beginning of real freedom!

Then I heard your broadcasts on being under a curse without really knowing it and prayed with you as you prayed the prayer of release from curses. Now I am free!

It is as if a dam has broken and God can move in my spirit. The blockage is gone and I have grown so much spiritually in a few weeks that I can only praise Him for His blessing. Sometimes I weep when I think about all He has done and is doing for me, and it is such a relief to be able to relax.

Truly, we worship a wonderful God!

Questions for the Study ————————————————

1. What are the two forces that the Bible states can determine the outcome of an individual's walk in life?
2. Can success elude someone who works hard, gets advanced schooling or thinks positively? If so, what is one main reason?
3. Can curses be generational? Read Deuteronomy 28:45–46 and Exodus 20:3–5.
4. What is one word that can sum up the effects of a curse?
5. Does a curse affect only the person living under it?
6. Can a person under a curse still achieve success?
7. Sometimes curses may not have their origin in previous generations. What else may cause them?
8. If you feel you are under a curse, does this mean there is no hope for you?

Life Application ————————————————

1. Do you see yourself (or someone you know) living under the circumstances described in this chapter? What specifically do you see that might indicate that a curse is in operation?
2. How has this affected those around you (or around the person)?
3. Do you see any possible generational curses in operation in your family? If so, what specifically?
4. Is there an area of your life in which frustration is a recurring experience? If so, what is that area?
5. There is hope in the Lord. Read the two letters of encouragement on pages 21–22.

Memory Verse ───────────────────────

"Behold, I set before you today a blessing and a curse: the blessing, if you obey the commandments of the LORD your God which I command you today."

Deuteronomy 11:26–27

Faith Response ───────────────────────

Lord, because I desire to be blessed, I choose this day to obey Your Word and to live my life following the example You set for us.

Answers

1. Blessings and curses.
2. Yes, because there is a curse over that person.
3. Yes.
4. Frustration.
5. No, it can affect a family, a community or a nation.
6. Yes, though he or she is not able to enjoy it.
7. Deeds or events in your own lifetime.
8. No, because God has provided a remedy.

2

Invisible Barriers

In previous years I spent much time counseling people like those described in the previous chapter. But it was often a frustrating task. Certain people would progress spiritually up to a point, and then they seemed to encounter an invisible barrier. It was not that they lacked sincerity or dedication. In fact, they often seemed more sincere and dedicated than others who made better progress. They would accept the counsel I gave them and try to put it into practice, but the results were—to say the least—disappointing, both for them and for me.

After dealing with such a case, I would find myself praying, "Lord, why is it that I cannot better help this person? Is there something I don't understand—something more that I need to know?" After a while, I realized that God was answering my prayer. He began to draw aside a veil and to reveal a world of powerful forces that do not operate according to natural laws. The revelation did not come all at once, but step by step as I discerned a single thread running through a series of apparently unconnected incidents.

One key incident occurred when I was a guest speaker in a Presbyterian church. I had come to the end of my prepared message, and was uncertain how to proceed. As I remained standing behind the pulpit, I noticed a family—father, mother and teenage daughter—on the front row to my left. The thought came to me, *There is a curse over that family*. This was not related to the theme of my message, or to anything I had in mind at that time. Yet the impression would not leave me: *There is a curse over that family*.

Finally, after some moments of hesitation, I stepped out from behind the pulpit and went over to the father. I explained to him what I was feeling and asked if he would like me to revoke the curse and release the family from it in the name of Jesus. He replied immediately that he would. It was the first time I had ever done anything like this, and I was quite surprised that the man so readily accepted my statement. Only later did I come to understand why.

I stepped back behind the pulpit and said a brief prayer out loud, breaking the curse over the family. I was not touching any member of the family as I prayed, but when I concluded with the words *In the name of Jesus*, there was a distinct, visible, physical reaction in the whole family. A momentary shudder seemed to pass through each of them in turn.

At this point I noticed that the girl, who was about eighteen years old, had her left leg in a cast from above the thigh to the bottom of her foot. I went over to the father again and asked if he would like me to pray for his daughter's leg to be healed. Again he responded very positively, then added, "But you need to know that she has broken the same leg three times in eighteen months, and the doctors say it will not heal."

Today, such a statement—that a person had broken the same leg three times in eighteen months—would set off an alarm bell inside me, warning that a curse was at work. At the time, however, I did not see any connection between a curse and such an unnatural series of accidents. I merely picked up the leg in its cast, held it in my hands and prayed a simple prayer for healing.

Some weeks later I received a letter from the father, thanking me for what had happened. He said that when they took their daughter back to the clinic, a new X-ray showed that her leg had healed. Shortly afterward the cast was removed.

He also mentioned briefly a series of strange, unhappy incidents that had affected the life of his family, and this explained his readiness to acknowledge the need for the whole family to be released from a curse.

In the months that followed, my mind kept returning to this incident. I felt that there was something significant about the order in which the Holy Spirit had led me. First, He had revealed the curse over the family and had prompted me to revoke it. Only then had He released me to pray for the healing of the daughter's leg. If I had prayed for healing without first revoking the curse, would the leg have been healed?

The more I pondered this, the more I was convinced that the revoking of the curse was an essential prelude to the healing of the girl's leg. It was an invisible barrier that would have prevented the healing God wanted her to receive.

All this seemed to tie in somehow with an incident in my own life. In 1904 my maternal grandfather had commanded a British expeditionary force sent to suppress the Boxer Rebellion in China. He had returned with various specimens of Chinese art, which became family heirlooms. In 1970, at the death of my mother, some of them passed by inheritance to me.

One of the most interesting items was a set of four exquisitely embroidered dragons, which found a place of honor on the walls of our living room. Their blend of colors—mainly purple and scarlet—was typically Oriental. They had five claws on each foot, which—an expert informed me—indicated they were "imperial" dragons. And, because my grandfather had been very close to me, they brought back memories of my early years in their home.

About this time, I began to sense some kind of opposition—that I could not define or identify—to the success of my ministry. It manifested itself in various kinds of frustrations, apparently unrelated, but which produced a cumulative pressure against me. I encountered barriers of communication that had never been there before with people close to me. Others on whom I had been relying failed to keep their commitments. A substantial legacy from my mother's estate was delayed interminably by a lawyer's inefficiency.

Eventually I set aside a period for intensive prayer and fasting. Quite soon, I began to notice a change in my attitude toward the dragons. From time to time, as I looked at them, a question would form in my mind: *Who in the Bible is represented as a dragon?* I had no doubt about the answer: Satan.[1]

This question would be followed by another: *Is it appropriate for you, as a servant of Christ, to display in your home objects that typify Christ's great adversary, Satan?* Again, the answer was clear: *No!* My inner struggle continued for a while, but finally I got rid of the dragons. I did this as a simple act of obedience, without any ulterior motive.

At that period, I was serving as a Bible teacher to the Church at large, speaking to groups of various kinds throughout the United States. My income, which came from the honoraria I received, was just sufficient to cover the basic needs of my family. Shortly after I got rid of the dragons, however, my financial position underwent a dramatic improvement. Without any special planning on my part, or any significant change in the nature or scope of my ministry, my income more than doubled. Also my long-delayed legacy finally came through.

I began to wonder if there was some undiscovered principle that linked this unexpected improvement in my personal finances with the healing of the girl with the broken leg. In the case of the girl, a curse over her family had been an invisible barrier to healing. When the barrier had been removed, healing had followed. In my case, too, perhaps there had been an invisible barrier—not to physical healing, but to the financial prosperity that proved to be an important element in God's plan for my life.

The more I pondered this, the more certain I became that those embroidered dragons had brought a curse into my house. By disposing of them, I had released myself from the curse and opened myself up to the blessing God had planned for me.

These changes enabled me to buy a home, which was to play a decisive part in the subsequent extension of my ministry. Nine years later, I sold that house for more than three times as much as I had paid for it! This money came exactly at a time when God was challenging me to major new financial commitments.

That experience with the dragons gave me new insight into the passage in Deuteronomy 7:25–26 where Moses warned Israel against any association with the idolatrous nations of Canaan:

> "You shall burn the carved images of their gods with fire; you shall not covet the silver or gold that is on them, nor take it for yourselves, lest you be snared by it; for it is an abomination to the LORD your God. Nor shall you bring an abomination into your house, lest you be doomed to destruction like it. You shall utterly detest it and utterly abhor it, for it is an accursed thing."

My embroidered dragons were not carved images, but they certainly were images of a false god who had been worshiped for millennia in China. By bringing them into my home, I had unknowingly exposed myself—and my family with me—to a curse. How grateful I was to the Holy Spirit for opening my eyes to what was at stake!

This led me to make a systematic study of the Bible's teaching on both blessings and curses. I was surprised by how much the Bible has to say about them. Words for *bless* or *blessing* occur about 410 times—excluding instances where the word in the original text merely has the meaning of "happy" or "fortunate" (as, for instance, in the Beatitudes). The word *curse*, in various forms, occurs about 230 times. This caused me to reflect how little teaching I had ever heard on this theme in all the years of my Christian experience. In fact, I could not recall hearing even one message that dealt systematically with this whole subject.

As a result of my study, I began to teach about curses in my public ministry. Each time I did this, I was surprised both by the powerful impact this teaching produced and by the number of people who obviously needed to hear it. Tapes from some of these meetings were circulated to other groups, and astonishing reports came back to me. Often it seemed that the message had transformed not merely the lives of individuals, but even whole congregations. Eventually I released three cassettes entitled "Curses: Cause and Cure."

Subsequently, on a trip to South Africa, I met a Jewish lady who had come to acknowledge Jesus as her Messiah. This lady—whom I will call Miriam—personally described to my wife, Ruth, and me the miracle she had experienced through listening to those three tapes.

Miriam had been working as executive secretary for a businessman who was president of his own company. She had discovered that her employer and all the executives in the company were in some strange cult that was led by a female "guru."

One day Miriam's employer handed her a cassette and said, "Here are some blessings that our guru has pronounced over us. Please type them." As she began to type,

Miriam realized that the "blessings" were actually fortune-telling, with strong occult overtones. She explained to her employer that such things were contrary to her faith in the Lord Jesus and the Bible, and asked to be excused. Her employer was gracious and apologized for having asked her to do something against her conscience.

Almost immediately after this, Miriam began to develop acute pain in both hands. Her fingers curled up and became absolutely rigid. She was no longer able to carry out her tasks as a secretary. The pain was so intense that she could not sleep in the same bed as her husband, because every time he turned over, the movement of the bed caused unbearable agony in her fingers. X-ray diagnosis revealed that her problem was rheumatoid arthritis.

A Christian friend of Miriam's heard of her distress and brought her my tapes on "Curses" to listen to. Miriam was a rather sophisticated lady, skeptical about such things as curses, which she associated with the Middle Ages. She had wondered, however, if there was any connection between her refusal to type the "blessing" and the subsequent problem with her hands. Could it be that the guru had pronounced a curse on her? So she consented to listen, feeling like the proverbial drowning man "clutching at a straw."

When they reached the point in the third tape where I led people in a prayer of release from any curse over their lives, the cassette jammed. It would not go forward or backward, neither would it eject!

"Obviously, then, I can't pray the prayer!" Miriam responded.

Miriam's friend had previously typed out the concluding prayer of release, however, and had a copy with her. She insisted that Miriam read the prayer out loud. Once again Miriam's skepticism asserted itself. She could not see how reading words from a typed sheet could have any effect on the condition of her hands.

Eventually, however, Miriam yielded to her friend's insistence, and began to read the prayer out loud. As she did so, her fingers uncurled and became free. The pain ceased, and by the time she had finished reading the prayer, she was completely healed. The whole experience had lasted only a few minutes.

Later Miriam returned to her doctor, who had taken the first X-rays. A second set of X-rays revealed no trace of arthritis.

One feature of this incident is particularly significant. The prayer of release that Miriam read *made no reference to physical healing.* Her hands were healed solely as a result of praying for release from a curse.

Here was further, dramatic evidence that a curse can be a barrier to keep people from receiving healing. The same had been true of the girl with the broken leg. In my own case, on the other hand, an unsuspected curse had been keeping me from the level of prosperity that God had intended for me.

If a curse could be a barrier to blessings such as healing or prosperity, was it not possible—or even probable—that many other kinds of blessing were likewise being withheld for the same reason? It was on this basis that I set myself to seek the answers to three related questions:

First, how can we recognize that a curse is operating in our lives?

Second, what must we do to revoke a curse and release ourselves from its consequences?

Third, how can we enter into the blessing of God?

The results of my search are presented in the following pages.

Questions for the Study

1. True or false: Only those people who lack sincerity and dedication face an invisible barrier to progress.
2. Powerful spiritual forces do not operate under what type of laws?
3. When Derek was praying over the family under a curse, what spoken words were used that caused a distinct physical reaction among them?
4. True or false: Revoking the curse over this family was not essential for the healing of the daughter's leg.
5. In Derek's own life, what items brought into his household caused a financial curse on him and his ministry? Read Deuteronomy 7:25–26.
6. Why were the dragons an abomination to the Lord?
7. In the story about Miriam's healing, what was the one significant feature about the prayer of release she read?

Life Application

1. Have you felt as if an invisible wall has stopped you from receiving the Lord's blessings? After reading chapters 1 and 2, do you have any insight as to what that invisible wall is?
2. Do you know of any items in your house or on your person that may have brought a curse to you or your household? Are you willing to remove them? Why or why not?

Memory Verse ———————————————————

Happy is the man who finds wisdom, and the man who gains understanding.

Proverbs 3:13

Faith Response ——————————————————

Lord, my heart is to walk in the truth. Give me the faith to apply what I learn.

Answers

1. False. Often it is the most sincere and dedicated who cannot progress.
2. Natural laws.
3. "In the name of Jesus."
4. False. The curse was an invisible barrier to her healing.
5. Four embroidered dragons.
6. Because they were an image of a false god that is worshiped in China. Also, the dragon in the Bible represents Satan.
7. No reference was made for physical healing, just release from a curse.

3

How Blessings and Curses Operate

The forces that determine history fall into two categories: visible and invisible. It is the interplay of these two realms that determines the course of history. As long as we confine our attention to things that are visible and material, we will find ourselves confronted from time to time by events and situations that we cannot fully explain or control.

To the visible realm belong all the normal objects and events of the material universe. We are all familiar with this realm and feel at home in it, even though events often do not follow the course we would wish. For many people, the limits of their awareness do not extend further. Yet the Bible opens a door to another, invisible realm, which is not material, but spiritual. The forces at work in this realm exercise a continuous and decisive influence on events in the visible realm.

In 2 Corinthians 4:17–18 Paul delineates these two realms:

For our light affliction, which is but for a moment, is working for us a far more exceeding and eternal weight of glory,
while we do not look at the things which are seen, but at
the things which are not seen. For the things which are
seen are temporary, but the things which are not seen are
eternal.

The things that belong to the visible realm are transitory
and impermanent. It is only in the invisible realm that we
can find true and abiding reality. It is in this realm, too,
that we discover the forces that will ultimately shape our
destiny, even in the visible realm. Paul makes it clear that
success in life depends upon being able to apprehend and
relate to that which is invisible and spiritual.

Both blessings and curses belong to the invisible, spiritual realm. They are vehicles of supernatural, spiritual
power. Blessings produce good and beneficial results; curses
produce bad and harmful results. Both are major themes
of Scripture. As already pointed out, the two words are
mentioned in the Bible more than 640 times.

Two important features are common to both. First, their
effect is seldom limited to the individual. It may extend to
families, tribes, communities or whole nations. Second,
once they are related, they tend to continue from generation to generation until something happens to cancel their
effects. A number of both blessings and curses mentioned
in the Bible in connection with the patriarchs have continued to work for nearly four thousand years and are still
at work today.

This second feature of blessings and curses has important practical implications. There may be forces at work
in our lives that have their origin in previous generations.
Consequently, we may be confronted with recurrent situations or patterns of behavior that cannot be explained
solely in terms of what has happened in our lifetimes or

personal experiences. The root cause may go back a long way in time, even thousands of years.

The main vehicle of both blessings and curses is *words*. Such words may be spoken or written or merely uttered inwardly. Scripture has much to say about the power of words. The book of Proverbs, in particular, contains many warnings as to how words may be used either for good or for evil. Here are just a few examples:

> The hypocrite with his mouth destroys his neighbor, but through knowledge the righteous will be delivered.
>
> Proverbs 11:9

> There is one who speaks like the piercings of a sword, but the tongue of the wise promotes health.
>
> Proverbs 12:18

> A wholesome tongue is a tree of life, but perverseness in it breaks the spirit.
>
> Proverbs 15:4

> Death and life are in the power of the tongue, and those who love it will eat its fruit.
>
> Proverbs 18:21

The apostle James also has much to say about the use of words. He points out that the tongue is a small member of the body, but the hardest of all to control:

> Even so the tongue is a little member and boasts great things. See how great a forest a little fire kindles! And the tongue is a fire, a world of iniquity. The tongue is so set among our members that it defiles the whole body, and sets on fire the course of nature; and it is set on fire by hell. . . .
>
> With it we bless our God and Father, and with it we curse men, who have been made in the similitude [likeness] of God.

37

Out of the same mouth proceed blessing and cursing.
My brethren, these things ought not to be so.

James 3:5–6, 9–10

James uses vivid imagery to emphasize the tremendous power that words have to affect people and situations, either for good or for evil. It is significant that he singles out both blessings and curses as words that can be charged with this kind of almost measureless power.

Words are not, however, the only channels through which the spiritual power of blessings and curses may be transmitted. There are various ways in which, at times, physical objects may become vehicles for this kind of power.

In Exodus 30:22–33 the Lord gave instructions to Moses for making a special anointing oil, which was to be used solely and exclusively for anointing the Tabernacle and its furniture, and also the priests who were to minister in the Tabernacle. In Leviticus 8:1–12 we read how this oil was applied. In verses 10–12 the account concludes:

Also Moses took the anointing oil, and anointed the tabernacle and all that was in it, and consecrated them. He sprinkled some of it on the altar seven times, anointed the altar and all its utensils, and the laver and its base, to consecrate them. And he poured some of the anointing oil on Aaron's head and anointed him, to consecrate him.

The word *consecrate* (or *sanctify*) in this passage means "to set apart to God, make holy." Thus the anointing oil became a vehicle to impart the blessing of holiness both to the Tabernacle and its furniture and to the priests who ministered in it.

Later in Israel's history, olive oil was used to impart appropriate blessing to the kings who were to rule the people on God's behalf. First Samuel 16:13 records how the prophet Samuel set David apart as God's chosen king:

"Then Samuel took the horn of oil and anointed him in the midst of his brothers; and the Spirit of the LORD came upon David from that day forward."

The oil poured on David's head by Samuel became a vehicle through which the blessing of the Holy Spirit was released in his life to equip him for his task as king.

In the New Testament, the emblems used in the Lord's Supper likewise become vehicles of God's blessing to those who partake of them. In 1 Corinthians 10:16 Paul says: "The cup of blessing which we bless, is it not the communion of the blood of Christ? The bread which we break, is it not the communion of the body of Christ?"

For those who partake with scriptural faith, these emblems transmit the blessing of God. Paul speaks specifically of "the cup of blessing"—that is, the cup that transmits the blessings of the new covenant to those who drink from it.

It must be emphasized, however, that in all the ordinances described above there is no room for "magic." The blessings are not inherent in the physical objects as such. They are imparted only to those who apprehend the will of God as revealed in Scripture, and who then by personal faith and obedience receive what is offered to them through the physical objects. Without faith and obedience, no blessing results.

On the contrary, in 1 Corinthians 11:29, Paul says concerning the emblems of the Lord's Supper: "He who eats and drinks in an unworthy manner eats and drinks judgment to himself." Such, then, are the alternatives. Faith and obedience receive God's blessing through the emblems; unbelief and disobedience provoke God's judgment. In both cases alike, it is the physical objects used in the Lord's Supper through which the spiritual power is transmitted, whether it be for blessing or for judgment.

Numbers 5:11–31 describes an ordinance used to determine whether a man's wife has been unfaithful to him or not. The appropriate prayers and sacrifices are required, but the focus of the ordinance is on a cup of water, into which the priest mixes dust from the floor of the Tabernacle and ink, which he scrapes from a written curse. The woman is then required to drink the water.

If she is guilty, the outworking of the written curse will be manifested in her physical body: "Her belly will swell, her thigh will rot, and the woman will become a curse among her people" (Numbers 5:27). That will be the punishment for her sin. In this case, the cup of water is the vehicle through which the curse is transmitted.

If the woman is innocent, on the other hand, she will not experience any harmful effects. In this way, God will have vindicated her righteousness, and her husband will not be free to bring any further accusation against her. Her innocence will have protected her from the curse.

The various instances given above establish one important scriptural truth: In certain circumstances, both blessings and curses can be transmitted through physical objects. On the other side, if we turn our attention from biblical practices to all the various forms of false religion and the occult, there is virtually no limit to the ways in which physical objects can become vehicles of curses.

In Exodus 20:4–5, in the second of the Ten Commandments, God explicitly forbids the making of any kind of idol or image for religious purposes, and He warns that those who break this commandment will bring judgment not only on themselves, but also on at least three following generations:

> "You shall not make for yourself a carved image—any likeness of anything that is in heaven above, or that is in the earth beneath, or that is in the water under the earth; you shall not bow down to them nor serve them. For I, the LORD your God, am a jealous God, visiting the iniquity of the fathers upon the children to the third and fourth generations of those who hate Me."

A wide range of objects comes under this ban. In my own case, which I have already described, the embroidered Chinese dragons exposed me to the invisible influence of a curse. It was true that I had no intention of worshiping them. Nevertheless, they represented something that had been an object of idolatrous worship for many centuries. They opened a channel into my home for the evil power of pagan worship that had been practiced for millennia.

Looking back later, I noticed one particular effect that those dragons had on me. Not merely were they a barrier that kept me from moving forward into the blessing of prosperity. They even kept me from seeing that the blessing was actually there. Only after I was free from their influence could I discern by faith what God had prepared for me.

Since that time, I have observed the same effect in the lives of many people under a curse. The curse not only keeps them from receiving the blessing God is offering to them. It also keeps them from realizing that the blessing is there to receive. Only when the Holy Spirit shines the light of Scripture into our lives do we begin to understand how the devil has been deceiving and cheating us.

Questions for the Study ───────────────

1. What are the two types of forces that determine history? *visible, invisible*
2. True or false: The things that belong to the invisible realm are transitory and impermanent. F
3. What are the two important features common to both blessings and curses? *vehicle of supernatural power*
4. What is the main vehicle for blessings and curses? *words*
5. True or false: Only words that are spoken have any power. F
6. Which book of the Bible contains many warnings *Proverbs* concerning the power of words for good or for evil?
7. Besides words, a physical object can be used in certain circumstances as a vehicle for blessings. Name an example of this given in the Bible. *oil, cup, bread*
8. True or false: A curse keeps people not only from receiving God's blessing but from realizing there is a blessing to receive. T

Life Application ───────────────

1. Blessings and curses, once released, tend to continue from generation to generation until something happens to cancel their effects. Ask the Holy Spirit to reveal to you if there are any generational curses affecting you or your family. If there are, what are they?
2. Go over the verses from Proverbs and James on pages 37–38 dealing with the use of words for good or evil. Do you think your life has been affected by good or evil words? What specifically has had an impact on you?
3. Have you ever spoken words that ministered death instead of life? If so, take a few moments and ask

the Lord to forgive you. If you are aware of specific situations, name them.

4. Physical items are often used in the occult to transmit curses. Read Exodus 20:4–5 for the Lord's warning to us concerning this type of disobedience.

Memory Verse ——————————————————————————

Death and life are in the power of the tongue, and those who love it will eat its fruit.

Proverbs 18:21

Faith Response ——————————————————————

Jesus, I choose this day to be a channel of blessings and not curses. Help me speak words of life instead of words of death.

Answers

1. Visible and invisible.
2. False. Only in the invisible realm can we find true and abiding reality.
3. Their effects are seldom limited to an individual; and both have important practical implications.
4. Words.
5. False. Powerful words can be spoken, written or uttered inwardly.
6. Proverbs.
7. Anointing oil used to sanctify and the elements of the Lord's Supper.
8. True.

4

Moses' List of Blessings and Curses

Some people are happy to accept the fact that blessings are valid, but are skeptical about curses, which they associate with superstitious practices from the Dark Ages. Such thinking is unrealistic. We cannot focus exclusively on one aspect of opposites because it is acceptable to us, and simply ignore the other because it is unacceptable. The opposite of hot is cold; both are real. The opposite of good is evil; both are real. In just the same way, blessings are real and so are curses.

My ministry brings me in touch with Christians from many different backgrounds in many different lands. I find that most of God's people do not know how to discern between blessings and curses. Many Christians who should be enjoying blessings are actually enduring curses. There are two main reasons for this: First, they simply do not know how to recognize what a blessing and a curse is, or how to discern them; second, if they are under a curse, they do not understand the basis upon which they can be released.

God is the sole and supreme source of all blessings, although they may come to us through many channels. Curses, too, often proceed from God, but He is not the sole source. Later on, we shall deal with other sources of curses.

The curses that proceed from God are one of His main ways of bringing judgment on the rebellious, the unbelieving and the ungodly. The history of the human race provides a long, sad record of the outworking of God's curses pronounced upon such people.

Over the years it has become fashionable to suggest that there is a dichotomy between the Old Testament and the New. According to this interpretation, the Old Testament depicts God as a God of wrath and judgment; the New depicts Him as a God of love and mercy. In fact, however, the two Testaments are consistent with each other. Each depicts God as being, at one and the same time, a God of mercy and of judgment.

The story of Jericho, related in Joshua 6, combines these two sides of God's dealings as vividly and dramatically as any passage in the New Testament. While the city of Jericho perished under one single, comprehensive judgment of God, the harlot Rahab, with her entire family, emerged unscathed. The record indicates, furthermore, that later Rahab became the wife of Salmon, one of the princes of Judah, and took her place in the genealogical line from which Israel's Messiah, Jesus, was to come! (See Matthew 1:5.)

In Romans 1:17–18 Paul explains that the Gospel contains the supreme revelation of these two aspects of God, His mercy and His judgment: "For in it [the Gospel] the righteousness of God is revealed from faith to faith. . . . For the wrath of God is revealed from heaven against all ungodliness and unrighteousness of men."

On the one hand, God's mercy offers His righteousness, which He imparts to those who receive by faith the substitutionary sacrifice of Jesus on their behalf. Yet, at the same time, this sacrifice is also the ultimate revelation of God's wrath, poured out upon Jesus when He became identified with man's sin. Christians who question the reality of God's judgment on sin should ponder afresh the significance of the crucifixion. Even Jesus could not make sin acceptable to God, but had to endure the full outpouring of His wrath.

Further on, in Romans 11:22, Paul again presents these two aspects of God's dealings side by side: "Therefore consider the goodness [or kindness] and severity of God." To obtain an accurate picture of God, we must always keep both aspects of His character before us. His blessings proceed out of His kindness, but His judgments proceed out of His severity. Both are equally real.

In Proverbs 26:2 Solomon makes it clear that there is always a reason for every curse: "Like a flitting sparrow, like a flying swallow, so a curse without cause shall not alight."

This principle has a double application. On the one hand, a curse cannot take effect unless there is a cause for it. On the other hand, the converse is also true. Wherever there is a curse at work, there is a cause for it. In seeking to help people obtain release from a curse, I have learned by experience that it is often helpful first to discover the cause.

The 68 verses of Deuteronomy 28, which are devoted solely to the theme of blessings and curses, reveal the primary cause of each. In verses 1 and 2 Moses deals first with the cause of blessings: "If you diligently obey the voice of the LORD your God, to observe carefully all His commandments . . . all these blessings shall come upon you and overtake you, because you obey the voice of the LORD your God."

More literally, the first part could be translated: "If you will listen listening to the voice of the Lord your God. . . ." The repetition of the verb *to listen* gives added emphasis. Simply stated, the conditions for enjoying the blessings are: first, listening to God's voice; second, doing what He says.

Throughout all dispensations, these have been the unchanging requirements for living in a covenant relationship with God. In Exodus 19:5, when God prepared to enter into His first covenant with Israel at Sinai, He said: "Now therefore, if you will indeed obey My voice and keep My covenant, then you shall be a special treasure to Me above all people." The basic requirements were to listen to God's voice and obey the terms of His covenant.

Under the New Covenant, in John 10:27, Jesus similarly described those whom He acknowledged as "His sheep"—that is, His true disciples: "My sheep hear My voice . . . and they follow Me." The basic requirements are still the same: hearing the Lord's voice and following Him in obedience.

Hearing the Lord's voice takes us beyond mere religious profession or formal observances. Nothing is more unique and distinctive than a person's voice. Hearing the Lord's voice implies an intimate relationship with Him in which He can speak to each one of us *personally*.

The Lord does not speak in this way to our physical ears or to our natural minds. His communication is Spirit-to-spirit—that is, by His Spirit to our spirit. Projected in this way, His voice penetrates to the innermost depths of our being. From there its vibrations are felt in every area of personality.

The Lord may speak in this way through the Bible, or He may impart a word of direct revelation. Merely reading the Bible, however, is not sufficient by itself, unless the words on its pages are transformed by the Holy Spirit into a living voice. It is only a relationship of this kind with God that truly qualifies us for the blessings He has promised to those *who hear and obey His voice*.

Further on, in Deuteronomy 28:15, Moses states the primary cause of all curses:

"But it shall come to pass, if you do not obey the voice of the LORD your God, to observe carefully all His commandments and His statutes which I command you today, that all these curses will come upon you and overtake you."

The cause of curses is exactly opposite to that of blessings. Blessings result from hearing God's voice and doing what He says. Curses result from *not* hearing God's voice and *not* doing what He says. This refusal to hear and obey God's voice can be summed up in one word: *rebellion*—not against man, but against God.

In Deuteronomy 28 Moses also gives comprehensive lists of the various forms that both blessings and curses take. The blessings are listed in verses 3 through 13, the curses in verses 16 through 68. Anyone who seeks to understand this whole subject should study this chapter carefully in its entirety.

Out of my own studies, I have attempted to make two lists that sum up the blessings and the curses in the order in which they are mentioned. My suggested list of blessings is as follows:

Exaltation
Health
Reproductiveness
Prosperity
Victory
God's favor

Reproductiveness is not a common English word, but it is intended to describe a condition in which every area of a person's life is fruitful and reproductive. This would include family, livestock, crops, business and the exercise of creative talents. All these should reflect God's blessing in appropriate ways.

48

In his list of curses in verses 16 through 68, Moses goes into much greater detail than with the blessings. Essentially, however, the curses are the opposite of the blessings. Here is my suggested summary:

Humiliation
Barrenness, unfruitfulness
Mental and physical sickness
Family breakdown
Poverty
Defeat
Oppression
Failure
God's disfavor

Earlier, in verse 13, Moses concludes his list of blessings with two vivid verbal pictures. Each of us would do well to consider how these pictures might apply in our own lives.

First, Moses says: "The LORD will make you the head and not the tail. . . ." I once asked the Lord to show me how this would apply in my life. I felt He gave me this answer: The head makes the decisions and the tail just gets dragged around.

It was left to me to decide which role I was playing. Was I acting like a head, in control of each situation, making the appropriate decisions and seeing them successfully carried out? Or was I merely playing the part of a tail, being dragged around by forces and circumstances I did not understand and could not control?

To drive his meaning home, Moses uses a second phrase: "You shall be above only, and not be beneath." This might be illustrated by a meeting between two Christian acquaintances.

"How are you doing?" the first asks.

"Under the circumstances," the second replies, "I'm not doing badly."

"I'm glad for that," the first one responds. "But whatever are you doing under the circumstances?"

These illustrations of Moses confront us with an opportunity for self-evaluation. Am I living like a head or a tail? Am I living under my circumstances, or above them? The answers we give will help us to see how much of God's blessing we are actually enjoying.

God's blessings	God's curses
exaltation	humiliation
health	barrenness
reproductiveness	unfruitfulness
prosperity	mental & physical sickness
victory	family breakdown
God's Favor	poverty
	defeat
	oppression
	failure
	God's disfavor

Questions for the Study ─────────────

1. One reason many Christians endure curses instead of blessings is that they do not know how to discern them. Name a second reason. *dk. how they can be released*
2. True or false: All blessings come from God, and some curses can also come from God. *T*
3. The Old and New Testament shows us that God is a God of both *mercy* and *judgment* Review Romans 11:22.
4. A curse cannot take effect unless there is a *cause* for it.
5. What is the primary cause for all curses? *rebellion. not hearing and not obeying God*
6. List the forms that blessings take. *reproductiveness*
7. List the categories into which curses fall.

Life Application ─────────────

1. Read Deuteronomy 28:1–6 and Deuteronomy 28:15–19.Working from the list of blessings, which ones do you see evident in your life?
2. Working from the list of curses, do you see any of them in operation in your life? If so, which ones?
3. What stands in the way of your hearing and obeying the Lord?
4. What can be done to remove these obstacles?

Memory Verse ─────────────

"I call heaven and earth as witnesses today against you, that I have set before you life and death, blessing and cursing; therefore choose life, that both you and your descendants may live."

Deuteronomy 30:19

Faith Response

Today, Lord, I choose life and not death, blessings and not curses. I choose to hear and obey Your Word. I submit myself to You, God, and I resist the devil (see James 4:7).

Answers

1. They do not know the basis of how to release blessings.
2. True.
3. Mercy, judgment.
4. Cause.
5. Not hearing and obeying God's voice—in other words, rebellion.
6. Exaltation, health, reproductiveness, prosperity, victory, God's favor.
7. Humiliation, barrenness, mental and physical sickness, family breakdown, poverty, defeat, oppression, failure, God's disfavor.

5

Seven Indications of a Curse

Through personal observation and experience, I compiled the following list of seven problems indicating that a curse is at work. When I compared my list with that of Moses, in Deuteronomy 28, I was impressed by the close correspondence between them.

1. Mental and/or emotional breakdown
2. Repeated or chronic sicknesses (especially if hereditary)
3. Barrenness, a tendency to miscarry or related female problems
4. Breakdown of marriage and family alienation
5. Continuing financial insufficiency
6. Being "accident-prone"
7. A history of suicides and unnatural or untimely deaths

The presence of only one or two of these problems would not necessarily be sufficient, by itself, to establish conclusively the working of a curse. But when several of the problems are present, or when any one of them tends to recur repeatedly, the probability of a curse increases proportionately. In the last resort, however, it is only the Holy Spirit who can provide an absolutely accurate "diagnosis."

1. Mental and/or emotional breakdown

The corresponding phrases from Deuteronomy 28 are: *madness, driven mad* (28, 34);[1] *confusion of heart* or *confusion of mind* (28); *a trembling heart* or *an anxious mind* (65); *anguish of soul* or *a despairing heart* (65).

The areas affected are described as the heart, the soul or the mind. In other words, the inner citadel of human personality has been breached by invading, hostile forces. Such people no longer have full control over their own thoughts and emotions and reactions. They may be "haunted" by an inner specter continually taunting them: "You're losing control. . . . There's no hope for you. . . . Your mother ended up in a mental institution, and you'll be next!"

I have been amazed to discover how many Christians are going through these inner struggles. Often they are reluctant to acknowledge their problem to others—or even to themselves—for fear that this would be a denial of their faith.

Two key words are *confusion* and *depression.* These almost invariably have their roots in some form of occult involvement. Often there is demonic activity. In most cases, however, it is necessary to deal with the occult involvement and to revoke the resulting curse before the demons can be driven out.

2. Repeated or chronic sicknesses (especially if hereditary)

The corresponding phrases from Deuteronomy 28 are numerous: *plague* or *plagued with diseases* (21); *consump-*

tion or *wasting disease* (22); *severe burning fever* (22); *in-flammation* (22); *incurable boils* (27, 35); *tumors* (27); *scabs* or *festering sores* (27); *incurable itch* (27); *blindness* (28); *extraordinary, fearful, prolonged plagues* (59); *serious and prolonged sicknesses* or *severe and lingering diseases* (59); *every other kind of sickness and plague* (61).

This list does not necessarily indicate that every form of sickness or disease is the direct result of a curse. There are, however, certain key words that occur: *plague, incurable, extraordinary, fearful, prolonged, lingering.* These serve as warning signals. They create what might be called "the atmosphere of a curse." They suggest evil, malevolent forces at work.

There is another common medical term that is not explicitly used in Deuteronomy 28, but has a similar connotation. It is *malignant* or *malignancy.* The primary definition of *malignant* in *Collins English Dictionary* is "having or showing desire to harm others." Obviously this describes a person, rather than a mere physical condition. Even more than the words in the previous paragraph, it suggests an evil, malevolent intelligence at work. Our use of such a term indicates an unconscious recognition that we are dealing with factors that are not purely physical.

Another very significant term used in reference to certain types of sickness is *hereditary.* It describes a condition that passes down from generation to generation. This is one of the commonest and most typical marks of a curse at work. For this reason, whenever I am asked to pray for someone who has a hereditary physical problem, I am always open to the possibility that I am confronting the effects of a curse.

At about the age of sixty, a friend of mine, who is a pastor, developed a condition diagnosed as hemochromatosis, a disease that causes the patient to produce too much iron in the blood, especially storing it in the vital organs, namely the liver and heart. His father had died of the same disease at age 67. The doctor pronounced it hereditary, incurable and life threatening. Every week he had to have phlebotomy (old-fashioned bloodletting).

After much prayer, especially by one of the prayer groups, my friend stood before his congregation in a Sunday morning service and made a simple, unemotional affirmation: "In the name of Jesus, I release myself from every evil inheritance from my father."

He was immediately and completely cured. Five years have passed since then. He has received no further treatment and there has been no recurrence of his problem.

In the foregoing comments, I have deliberately refrained from suggesting that any specific sickness is always, or necessarily, attributable to a curse. In many of the sicknesses mentioned, it would be highly probable that a curse is at work, but, without further evidence, it would be wrong to assert that this is necessarily so. There is only one "expert" whose diagnosis is final, and that is the Holy Spirit. We always need to be conscious of our dependence on Him.

3. Barrenness, a tendency to miscarry or related female problems

The key phrase here from Deuteronomy 28 is: "Cursed shall be the fruit of your body" or your womb (18). This curse may affect any of the various organs or functions involved in procreation. Ruth and I have ministered to hundreds of women whose infirmities came under the heading of "female problems." These included: inability to conceive; a tendency to miscarry; failure to menstruate; irregular menstruation; debilitating menstrual cramps; frigidity; cysts, tumors or other growths; or structural defects affecting any of the various organs connected with the reproductive process. Quite often this kind of curse affects whole families, with the result that all, or almost all, the females in a family may be afflicted with problems of this kind.

Ruth and I make it a principle not to minister to such people without first instructing them on the nature and causes of curses, and then praying with them for release. In many cases this has produced healing and wholeness in the affected areas or functions. Sometimes it proves sufficient merely to revoke the curse, without any specific prayer for healing.

The following letter illustrates the results that can follow when the curse of barrenness is revoked.

My husband and I had been married for twelve years and had not been able to have children. Medical tests revealed that there was nothing physically wrong with us.

On July 7, 1985, we attended a meeting in Amsterdam at which you were speaking. You taught on healing, and also reasons why people are not healed. As you began speaking on curses over families, the Lord spoke to my heart that this was a problem in my family. As you led everyone in a prayer for deliverance from any curse over their lives, I felt a definite sense of release from bondage.

When I came to the platform, you asked me to fetch my husband for prayer also. Then as you prayed for us, you pronounced that the curse over my life had been broken, and as Ruth laid hands on my womb, she spoke that I would be "neither barren nor unfruitful." The whole congregation was asked to stand and join in prayer for us. Following that meeting, my husband and I both felt strongly that the Lord had heard our prayers.

About two and a half years later, in another public meeting in England, this couple came up to show us the beautiful baby boy who was the manifestation of the blessing that had replaced the curse of barrenness over their lives.

The connection between menstrual problems and a curse is brought out in another letter, dated December 22, 1987, from a Christian lady in her thirties serving the Lord in Southeast Asia:

In 1985 I borrowed a set of tapes that had been recorded in Singapore, among which was the message by Derek Prince on "Blessings and Cursings." After listening to this message one night in my room I stood in the darkness to say the prayer on the end of the tape even though I was not aware of anything in particular. I just thought, *If there is something, I want to be free from it.*

I didn't immediately become aware of any change, although something did happen, the significance of which didn't strike me until later. The Lord prompted me shortly after this to make a note in my diary when I had my period. This was something I had never done before as I'd not had regular periods since the time they first began at age thirteen. Therefore there had been little point in keeping a record. My periods in fact had been so irregular that I'd even gone six or eight or ten months at a time without having one at all.

I'd been to doctors about this in my twenties and had been given medication (without result) and much unwise and ungodly advice.

I had prayed about my condition but not too seriously—possibly because I was single—but I had been told that I would experience a certain amount of discomfort and irregularity in my metabolism due to hormonal imbalance until this condition was corrected.

On listening to the tape again a few months later, I was struck by Derek Prince's statement that "almost all, if not all, menstrual disorders are a result of a curse." I realized as I reached for my diary and checked the dates that I'd been perfectly regular (28-day cycles) since praying the prayer in August 1985. I was amazed to realize I was healed and that it had been the Lord who had prompted me to write down the dates of my periods.

As I reflected on my life, questioning where "the curse" could have come in, since no curse can alight without a cause, I remembered how throughout my high school years (ages 13–17) menstruation was generally referred to as "the curse" by me and my peers. Surely that confirms that "death and life are in the power of the tongue" (Proverbs 18:21).

Since that time in August '85 I have regularly kept a record and found my cycle to be consistently 27–29 days. Also, my weight which previously fluctuated has remained stable.

It is important to notice that—like Miriam in chapter 2—this lady did not pray for physical healing. She simply released herself from a curse, and healing followed as a consequence.

In this area of the procreative functions there is another common indication of a curse at work: an infant born with the umbilical cord wrapped around its neck—sometimes more than once. Quite often, of course, this can result in a stillbirth—thus causing death where there should be a new life.

4. Breakdown of marriage and family alienation

One effect of the curse in this area is described in Deuteronomy 28:41: "You shall beget sons and daughters, but they shall not be yours; for they shall go into captivity." Countless parents in the present generation have experienced this curse. They have seen their sons and daughters taken captive by a rebellious subculture devoted to drugs, sex, satanic music and every form of the occult.

In Malachi 4:5–6 the prophet paints a grim picture of conditions in the world just before this age closes:

"Behold, I will send you Elijah the prophet before the coming of the great and dreadful day of the LORD. And he will turn the hearts of the fathers to the children, and the hearts of the children to their fathers, lest I come and strike the earth with a curse."

59

Malachi depicts an evil force at work, alienating parents from children and producing a breakdown of family relationships. Unless God intervenes, he warns, this curse that is destroying family life will be extended to the whole earth, bringing disaster in its train.

Malachi has put his finger on the most urgent social problem of our contemporary culture. We need to see it as the outworking of a curse, which is responsible for the agonies of strife-torn homes, broken marriages and disintegrated families. Perhaps the most accurate word to describe the force responsible for these results is *alienation*. It comes between husbands and wives, parents and children, brothers and sisters, and all others who should be united by the bonds of family. Its goal is the destruction of the family.

Nevertheless for those who will accept God's counsel, the situation is not hopeless. There is a remedy. First we must face the fact that a curse is at work. Then we must take the steps indicated by Scripture to revoke the curse and release its captives. I have seen families transformed and restored by these means.

5. Continuing financial insufficiency

Two related phrases from Deuteronomy 28 are: "Cursed shall be your basket and your kneading bowl" or trough (17); "you shall not prosper in your ways" or you will be unsuccessful in everything you do (29).

The full outworking of this curse, however, is most graphically presented in verses 47–48:

> "Because you did not serve the Lord your God with joy and gladness of heart, for the abundance of everything, therefore you shall serve your enemies, whom the Lord will send against you, in hunger, in thirst, in nakedness, and in need of everything."

Moses here presents two opposite alternatives. Verse 47 describes God's will for His obedient people: to "serve the LORD your God with joy and gladness of heart, for the abundance of everything." The NIV renders this: to "serve the LORD your God joyfully and gladly in the time of prosperity."

Verse 48 describes the curse that will come on God's people if they are disobedient: to "serve your enemies, whom the LORD will send against you, in hunger, in thirst, in nakedness, and in need of everything." Consider what is depicted in this verse: hunger, thirst, nakedness and need of all things. Combine all four elements into one situation, and the result can be defined in a single phrase: *absolute poverty.*

Taken together, verses 47 and 48 point to a simple conclusion: Prosperity is a blessing and poverty is a curse.

Over the centuries, however, a tradition has developed within the Christian Church that poverty is a blessing. Certainly God has great compassion on the poor, and Christians should have the same attitude and be willing to make great personal sacrifices on their behalf. But Scripture never suggests that God *inflicts* poverty as a blessing upon His believing people.

In this respect, the revelation of the New Testament harmonizes with that of the Old. In 2 Corinthians 9:8 Paul sums up the abundance of God's provision for Christians: "And God is able to make all grace abound toward you, that you, always having all sufficiency in all things, may have an abundance for every good work."

In this one terse sentence Paul doubles and redoubles his words to emphasize the generosity of God's provision for His people. The word *abound* or *abundance* occurs twice. The word *all*—or its equivalent—occurs five times: *all* grace . . . *always* . . . *all* sufficiency in *all* things . . . *every* good work. Such is the measure of God's provision. It transcends mere sufficiency and lifts us to a level of abundance, where we have something over and above our own needs and can minister to the needs of others.

It would be unscriptural, however, to interpret poverty and abundance by the materialistic standards of contemporary Western civilization. In John 6:38 Jesus revealed the motivation of His life on earth: "For I have come down from heaven, not to do My own will, but the will of Him who sent Me." The motivation of the disciple must be the same as that of the Master: *to do God's will.*

It is from this perspective that "poverty" and "abundance" must be defined. Poverty is having less than all you need to do God's will in your life. The greater the gap between what you need and what you have, the greater the degree of poverty. Abundance, on the other hand, is having all you need to do God's will—and something over to give to others. God's abundance is not provided for us to squander on carnal self-indulgence, but *for every good work*, that is, sharing with others the blessings of grace that have enriched our own lives.

When poverty and abundance are interpreted in this way, it follows that there is no absolute standard that can be applied to all Christians. The standard for each believer must be determined in relation to *the will of God for his or her life*.

These conclusions about poverty and abundance need to be further qualified in two ways. First, we must recognize that faith to appropriate God's abundance is certain to be tested. There may be periods when we have to content ourselves with the barest sufficiency. Such periods, however, should be temporary. Once our motives have been purified and our faith has stood the test, God will release His abundance in the measure that He can trust us to use for His glory.

Second, we must recognize also that there is a higher level of wealth than just the material. When Moses turned his back on the wealth and luxury of Egypt and settled in a remote corner of a desert, the writer of Hebrews says that he esteemed "the reproach of Christ *greater riches* than the treasures in Egypt" (Hebrews 11:26, emphasis added). Moses did not settle for poverty. He exchanged material riches for riches of a higher order.

In the same way today, there is the kind of Christian who renounced material wealth deliberately in order to serve God in a situation where wealth would be an encumbrance. Often this is a prerequisite for identifying with the poor and oppressed of the earth. In Proverbs 13:7 Solomon contrasts such a person with one whose only wealth is material: "There is one who makes himself rich, yet has nothing; and one who makes himself poor, yet has great riches."

There are also many Christians in our day who are enduring affliction and persecution for Christ's sake. They may be deprived of everything that could be described as material wealth, but in its place they are heirs to wealth of a higher order.

Nevertheless, this does not alter the basic nature of persistent material poverty. Where this is not the direct outcome of commitment to Christ, it is normally a mark of a curse, whether it affects an individual, a family or a larger social group.

6. Being "accident-prone"

This phrase describes a person who is unnaturally prone to personal accidents. Deuteronomy 28 contains no specific mention of this, although it is hinted at in the phrase "you shall grope . . . as a blind man gropes in darkness" (29).

One characteristic effect of this curse might be seen in what are called "freak" accidents. The girl described in chapter 2, who had broken the same leg three times in eighteen months, would be an obvious example.

To take another example, some people are good drivers, yet they have an abnormally high number of automobile accidents. In most cases, perhaps, it may be the fault of "the other driver." Nevertheless, the accidents still happen. A typical comment that identifies this kind of person would be, "Why does it always happen to me?"

Here are further examples, chosen more or less at random, of types of accidents that might indicate a curse at work: breaking an ankle through stepping off a curb; breaking a tooth on a soft piece of fruit; shutting a car door on a finger (here again, it may be "the other person"); slipping on a stair and falling headlong down a whole flight, with multiple injuries; swallowing a fish bone and choking on it; an insect in the eye causing some rare infection; being struck in the face by a stone thrown up by a passing car; a surgeon's error on the operating table resulting in permanent disability . . . the list could be endless.

It almost seems that there is an invisible, malicious force working against such people. At critical moments, it trips them, or causes them to stumble, or impels them to make a rash, unpremeditated move. Typically, such a person will exclaim, "I don't know what made me do that!" A remark of this kind is very revealing. It indicates that the person is aware that his actions are not entirely under his own control, but are affected by a nameless influence he cannot identify and against which he has no way of protecting himself.

The recognition of this type of problem is not purely subjective. It can be determined by statistical analysis. Some insurance companies use this kind of analysis to identify people who would be unusually high risks for insurance. They set their premiums accordingly.

7. A history of suicides and unnatural or untimely deaths

The references to unnatural or untimely death in Deuteronomy 28 are too numerous to itemize. A curse that takes this form affects not just a single individual but a larger social unit, such as a family or tribe. Normally, too, it continues from one generation to another. Many different cultures have recognized a force at work in human history that pursues the members of a family or a clan relentlessly until it finally destroys them. The ancient Greeks gave it the status of a "goddess," whom they named Nemesis. Other cultures have used different terminologies. Beneath the pagan overtones is an objective reality.

Quite often people who are affected by this type of curse experience a strong foreboding. They sense something dark and evil in the road ahead, but they do not know how to avoid it. A typical comment might be: "Well, it happened to my father, and I suppose I'm next on the list."

One common symptom of a curse of this kind is that people set dates for their own deaths. "I know I'll never live to see forty-five," they may say. Or, "All the men in my family die young." They imply, if they do not actually say, that this will be their fate, too. They have a kind of negative faith that embraces death, but refuses life.

The above list of seven indications of a curse is by no means exhaustive. Others could be added. You have probably read far enough by now, however, to take stock of your situation.

Various reactions are possible. You may, for example, no longer have any doubt about the nature of your problem. You have clearly identified one or more indications of a curse that apply to your life or to that of your family.

Alternatively, you may have an uneasy sense that a curse is at work, but you cannot pinpoint the precise form that it takes. You feel like the kind of person described in chapter 1. You have sensed the dark shadow from the past, but you do not know its source. Or you have seen that long, evil arm at work in various situations, but it operates behind a veil that you have not been able to tear aside.

In either case, you will be asking yourself, *How could such a thing happen to me? What is the source of my problem?*

This means that it is time for you to move on to Section 2: "No Curse without a Cause." This section explains many of the most common sources of a curse. If you can once discover the cause of your particular problem, you will be in a much better position to deal with it effectively.

Questions for the Study

1. True or false: The presence of one or two problems indicating a curse does not necessarily mean that one is under a curse. *T*

2. Two key words for *Mental and/or emotional breakdown* are *depression* and *confusion.* This type of curse usually has its roots in the *occult.*

3. Under *Repeated or chronic sicknesses*, what are the most common and typical marks of a curse at work? *hereditary*

4. True or false: Barrenness usually affects only a small number of women in a family. *F*

5. Under *Breakdown of marriage and family alienation*, what is the most accurate word to describe the force of such results? Its goal is the *destruction alienation* the family.

6. Under *Continuing financial insufficiency*, we discover that *prosperity* is a blessing and *poverty* is a curse. Read Deuteronomy 28:47–48.

7. True or false: Poverty and abundance should be judged by the standards of Western contemporary culture. *F*

8. One characteristic of being accident-prone is having *freak* accidents.

9. True or false: Under *History of suicides and unnatural or untimely deaths*, a person often experiences a strong feeling of foreboding. *T*

10. Most people under this curse have a *negative* faith that *embraces* death, but *refuses* life.

Life Application

1. Write down names of known family members from both parents' sides who have experienced one of the above curses.

2. After completing this list, look for generational occurrences in your family.
3. Do you see any indication of these curses operating in your life? How?
4. Ask the Holy Spirit to help you discover the cause of this problem, so it can be dealt with effectively.

Memory Verse ───────────────────────

God is able to make all grace abound toward you, that you, always having all sufficiency in all things, may have an abundance for every good work.

2 Corinthians 9:8

Faith Response ───────────────────────

Lord, I desire to be set free from any curses over my life. I will do whatever it takes to be delivered from them and walk in the freedom You purchased for me.

Answers

1. True. Only the Holy Spirit can provide an accurate diagnosis.
2. Confusion, depression; occult.
3. Hereditary problems.
4. False. It usually affects all or almost all of the women.
5. Alienation; destruction.
6. Prosperity, poverty.
7. False. The standard is determined in relation to the will of God for each believer's life.
8. Freak.
9. True.
10. Negative, embraces, refuses.

Section 2

No Curse without a Cause

Introduction

The operation of blessings and curses in our lives is not haphazard or unpredictable. On the contrary, both of them operate according to eternal, unchanging laws. It is to the Bible, once again, that we must look for a correct understanding of these laws.

In Proverbs 26:2 Solomon establishes this principle with respect to curses: "A curse without cause shall not alight." Behind every curse that comes upon us, there is a cause. If it seems that we are under a curse, we should seek to determine its cause. Then we shall be in a position to take appropriate action against it. This will also silence that nagging question, "Why do things like this always happen to me?"

This section lays bare the causes of the main curses that commonly afflict our lives. After reading it, you will be better able to understand and apply God's remedy, which is unfolded in the following section.

> My family on my father's side was under a bad curse that had to be broken. The curse had killed three children in our family. My older brother's oldest child was killed in a car wreck. My second child was also killed in a car wreck. My younger brother's third child fell off a horse and was killed when her head hit a rock. My younger sister's fourth child was diagnosed with an inoperable malignant brain tumor. Because her father was stationed in the Air Force, she came to live with me while receiving medical treatment. I broke the curse over her and she is alive and well today. I have prayed prayers of release until there couldn't be a demon brave enough to come within a block of our house!
>
> J. B.

6

False Gods

In the preceding chapters we have established two important facts concerning curses that proceed from God. First, they are one of the main ways in which He brings judgment on the rebellious and the ungodly. Second, the basic cause of such curses is the failure to hear God's voice and do what He says—or, in one simple word, *disobedience*.

Disobedience can take many forms. It is natural, therefore, to ask, What are some of the main forms of disobedience that particularly provoke God's curse?

The Bible leaves no doubt about the answer. The form of disobedience that most surely and inevitably provokes God's curse is the breaking of the first two of the Ten Commandments, which are stated in Exodus 20:1–5:

And God spoke all these words, saying:
"I am the Lord your God, who brought you out of the land of Egypt, out of the house of bondage.
"You shall have no other gods before Me.
"You shall not make for yourself a carved image—any likeness of anything that is in heaven above, or that is in

the earth beneath, or that is in the water under the earth; you shall not bow down to them nor serve them. For I, the LORD your God, am a jealous God, visiting the iniquity of the fathers upon the children to the third and fourth generations of those who hate Me."

What are the two sins God specifies here? The first is acknowledging any other god before—or besides—the Lord. It is not enough to acknowledge the Lord as the first or greatest of all gods. We must acknowledge that He is *the only true God*. There is no other besides Him.

In Isaiah 45:21 the Lord declares with great emphasis: "There is no other God besides Me, a just God and a Savior; there is none besides Me."

The second sin, described in the next commandment, is the making of any artificial representation of God and offering worship to it. In Romans 1:20–23 Paul analyzes what is involved in the breaking of these two commandments:

> For since the creation of the world God's invisible qualities— his eternal power and divine nature—have been clearly seen, being understood from what has been made, so that men are without excuse.
>
> For although they knew God, they neither glorified him as God nor gave thanks to him, but their thinking became futile and their foolish hearts were darkened. Although they claimed to be wise, they became fools and exchanged the glory of the immortal God for images made to look like mortal man and birds and animals and reptiles.
>
> NIV

Those who acknowledge false gods and practice idol worship have deliberately rejected the clear revelation of God available to them through creation. Instead, they have chosen to worship idols that become progressively debased. First, they take human form, but from there they descend to birds, then to animals and finally to reptiles. This exactly describes the practice of ancient Egypt. Three of their main gods were the vulture, the jackal and the cobra.

Our human minds are slow to understand the awful wickedness of idol worship. The true God, revealed first in creation and then more fully in Scripture, is holy, awesome, glorious, omnipotent. To represent Him in the likeness of any created being—whether human or animal—is to offer Him a deliberate insult. It is a calculated provocation of His wrath.

Let me illustrate this by a crude example. Suppose someone were to find a cockroach crawling on the floor, photograph it and then display the photograph over the title *Derek Prince*. I would surely interpret this as an insult aimed deliberately at me. How immeasurably worse is the insult offered to God by those who give His name not merely to the noblest of His creatures, but even to the most debased!

God's judgment on the breaking of these first two commandments bears the characteristic mark of a curse: It continues from generation to generation, at least as far as the fourth generation. In some nations and some cultures, the practice of worshiping false gods goes back over hundreds and even thousands of years, compounding the effect many times over.

A person who comes from such a background is heir to a curse that may be compared to a weed planted in his life, linking him to satanic forces outside himself. This weed has two kinds of roots: one long tap root going straight downward, and other less powerful lateral roots stretching out in various directions. The tap root represents the influence of ancestors who worshiped false gods. The lateral roots represent other influences to which the person has been exposed in his own lifetime, either through various sins he has committed or through his own attachment to false gods or in various other ways.

Before he can enjoy true liberty and the fullness of the new creation in Christ, this weed must be completely pulled out, with all its roots. The most important root, and the one hardest to deal with, is the tap root that links him to many generations who have worshiped false gods. Nothing but the supernatural grace and power of God can effectively remove all these roots. But thank God, there is hope in the promise of Jesus in Matthew 15:13: "Every plant which My heavenly Father has not planted will be uprooted."

The sins that bring this generational curse, however, do not stop short at the more obvious forms of idolatry. They include a second, wider range of practices that are not necessarily openly idolatrous, or even religious. Because their true nature is concealed by deceptive terminology, they are appropriately described as *occult* (derived from a Latin word meaning "hidden" or "covered over"). These occult practices have always held a powerful fascination[1] for fallen man, never more so than in the present generation.

Two of the strongest cravings of human nature are the desire for knowledge and the desire for power. Up to a certain point, man is able to satisfy these cravings from natural sources and by natural means. If he is not fully satisfied by what he obtains in this way, he will turn inevitably to supernatural sources. It is at this point that he easily becomes entrapped in the occult.

The reason for this is that there are actually only two available sources of supernatural knowledge and power in the universe: either God or Satan. Every form of supernatural knowledge or power that does not proceed from God, therefore, necessarily proceeds from Satan. If derived from God, it is legitimate; if derived from Satan, it is illegitimate.

Since God's Kingdom is the Kingdom of light, His servants know whom they are serving and what they are doing. On the other hand, since Satan's kingdom is a kingdom of darkness, most of those in his kingdom do not know the true identity of the one whom they are serving, or the true nature of what they are doing.

It was this craving for illegitimate knowledge that prompted man's first transgression in the Garden of Eden. God had set an invisible boundary between him and the tree of knowledge of good and evil. When man crossed this boundary, he found himself in Satan's territory and became a captive of Satan. Ever since then, the same kind of craving for illegitimate knowledge or power has continually lured men into an area where Satan is able to take them captive at his will (see 2 Timothy 2:26). As already stated, the generic name for this area is the occult.

Those who trespass in this area are seeking from Satan the supernatural knowledge or power that God does not permit man to seek from any other source but Himself. In so doing, they are, in fact, acknowledging Satan as a god besides the one true God, and are thus breaking the first of the Ten Commandants. In this way they are exposing themselves to the curse God has pronounced on all who break this commandment—a curse that extends as far as the fourth generation.

This conclusion is so important that it needs to be reemphasized: *All who become involved in the occult are exposing themselves to the curse pronounced on those who break the first commandment.*

In various passages the Bible describes the act of turning to false gods as "spiritual adultery," and condemns it as an even greater sin than physical adultery. Understood in this way, the warnings given in the book of Proverbs against involvement with an "immoral woman"—or an adulteress—apply to involvement in the occult. In Proverbs 5:3–6 this immoral woman is depicted as alluring and fascinating in her initial approaches, yet causing final ruin to those whom she seduces:

> For the lips of an immoral woman drip honey, and her mouth is smoother than oil; but in the end she is bitter as wormwood, sharp as a two-edged sword. Her feet go down

to death, her steps lay hold of hell. Lest you ponder her path of life—her ways are unstable; you do not know them.

The final statement is particularly illuminating: "Her ways are unstable; you do not know them." No limit can be set to the forms of deception practiced in the occult. As soon as one is exposed, another emerges in its place. It is, therefore, impossible to give a complete or definitive list of the various types of occult practices. It is, however, possible to identify and briefly describe the following three main branches: witchcraft, divination and sorcery.

Witchcraft is the *power* branch of the occult. Its root is exposed by a brief statement in 1 Samuel 15:23: "For *rebellion* is as the sin of witchcraft" (emphasis added). Witchcraft is an expression of man's rebellion against God. It is man's attempt to gain his own ends without submitting to God's Law. Its driving force is a desire to control people and circumstances. To gain this end it may use either psychological pressures or psychic techniques, or a combination of both.

There are three key words that expose the activity of witchcraft: *manipulate, intimidate, dominate.* Domination is its ultimate purpose. Manipulation and intimidation are alternative ways of achieving this purpose. Wherever people use verbal or nonverbal tactics to manipulate, intimidate and dominate those around them, witchcraft is at work.

In its simplest form, witchcraft is merely an expression of the corrupt, rebellious nature of fallen humanity. In Galatians 5:19–20, in the King James Version, it is listed—with idolatry—among "the works of the flesh." There are probably few people who have not resorted at some time or other to witchcraft in this form.

This is only the tip of the iceberg, however. It is characteristic of Satan that he exploits this "work of the flesh" as an opening for supernatural, demonic power that emanates from the kingdom of darkness. Through this opening, he moves in and takes control of men and women, making them tools of his evil purposes and slaves of his kingdom. The result is witchcraft practiced as an occult art, operating primarily through spells and curses.

The other two forms of the occult—divination and sorcery—are motivated by the same basic desire: to control people and circumstances.

Divination is the *knowledge* branch of the occult, offering many different forms of knowledge that cannot be obtained by purely natural means. In its commonest form, as *fortune-telling*, it offers supernatural knowledge of the future. It also includes all false forms of religious revelation that claim a supernatural source.

Sorcery operates through *material objects* or through other ways of impacting the physical senses, such as *drugs* or *music*. In Revelation 9:21 the word for *sorceries* is directly derived from the Greek word for *drugs*. In 2 Timothy 3:13 Paul warns that at the close of this age "evil men and impostors will grow worse and worse, deceiving and being deceived." The word translated *impostors* means literally "enchanters." Chanting—or incantation—has always been a technique of sorcery. The contemporary drug culture, with its accompaniment of "heavy metal" rock music, is a vivid example of two forms of sorcery working together.

The following is a brief list of various categories under which the "tools" of sorcery may be classified:

Any objects associated with idolatrous worship, whether pagan or professing to be Christian.

Any objects representing any kind of false religion or cult or satanic practice.

Any objects upon which a practitioner of the occult has invoked supernatural power. (Even if this power is ostensibly directed toward a "good" purpose, such as healing, its source makes it the channel of a curse.)

Any objects that are the expression of superstition, such as horseshoes, "lucky" coins, figures of "saints" and so on.

The following are some specific forms of the occult prevalent in our contemporary culture:

1. The power branch of the occult

Acupressure, acupuncture, astral projection, hypnosis, levitation, martial arts (those that invoke supernatural spiritual power), mind control, mind dynamics, parakinesis, table-tipping, telekinesis, "touch" healing, witchcraft.

2. The knowledge branch of the occult

Astrology, automatic writing, "channeling," clairaudience (hearing "voices"), clairvoyance, crystal balls, diagnosing by color therapy or a pendulum, divining, ESP, handwriting analysis, horoscopes, iridology, kabbala, mediums, mind reading, numerology, omens, palm reading, phrenology, séances, tarot cards, tea-leaf reading, telepathy, "witching." Also, all books that teach occult practices.

Also included under this heading are all false religions or cults that claim supernatural revelation but contradict the Bible. Distinguishing between true and false in this realm is like distinguishing between straight and crooked in the natural realm. Once we have established a standard of what is straight, we know that anything departing from that standard is crooked. It makes no difference whether it varies by one degree or by ninety degrees. It is crooked.

In the spiritual realm, the Bible is the standard of that which is *straight*—that is, *true*. Anything that departs from the Bible is *false*. Whether it departs by little or much is relatively unimportant. Some of the subtlest deceptions are those that appear to differ only a little from the Bible.

Particularly dangerous are religions that misrepresent the Person, the nature or the redemptive work of Jesus Christ. The New Testament, for example, presents Jesus as "God manifest in the flesh," but Jehovah's Witnesses teach that He was a created being. Again, Islam rejects the claim of Jesus to be the Son of God, and denies that He ever actually died on the cross. Yet the atoning death of Jesus is the only basis on which man can claim forgiveness of sins.

The following are some of the many false religions or cults that are active today: Anthroposophy, Black Mass, Children of God, Christadelphians, Christian Science, Freemasonry, Inner Peace Movement, Jehovah's Witnesses (Dawn Bible Students), Mormons (Church of Jesus Christ of Latter-Day Saints), New Age Movement, Religious Science, Rosicrucianism, Scientology, Spiritual Frontiers Fellowship, Spiritualism, Theosophy, Unification Church (Moonies, One World Crusade), Unitarian Church.

Also, Eastern religions or cults, such as Baha'i, Buddhism, Confucianism, Divine Light Mission, gurus, Hare Krishna, Hinduism, Islam, Shintoism, Transcendental Meditation, yoga.

3. The branch of the occult operating through physical objects, etc.

Amulets, ankhs (an ankh is a cross with a ring at the top), birthstones, charms (e.g., for wart removal), crystals used for healing, hallucinogenic drugs, "heavy metal" rock records or cassettes, hex signs, "lucky" symbols (e.g., inverted horseshoes), Ouija boards, pagan fetishes or religious artifacts, planchettes, talismans, zodiac charms.

God's estimate of those who are involved in the kinds of practice listed above is stated plainly in Deuteronomy 18:10–13:

> Let no one be found among you who sacrifices his son or daughter in the fire, who practices divination or sorcery, interprets omens, engages in witchcraft, or casts spells, or who is a medium or spiritist or who consults the dead. Anyone who does these things is detestable to the LORD, and because of these detestable practices the LORD your God will drive out those nations before you. You must be blameless before the LORD your God.
>
> NIV

Notice that those who engage in these occult practices are classed in the same category with those who sacrifice their children in fire to pagan gods. Under the Law of Moses, the mandatory penalty for all such practices was death.

It is important to recognize that *books* can be channels of occult power. When the professing Christians in Ephesus were confronted through the ministry of Paul with the reality of Satan's power, their reaction was dramatic:

> Many of those who believed now came and openly confessed their evil deeds. A number who had practiced sorcery brought their scrolls together and burned them publicly. When they calculated the value of the scrolls, the total came to fifty thousand drachmas.[2]
>
> Acts 19:18–19, NIV

The only appropriate way to deal with such occult material is to destroy it completely—by fire or by whatever means may be most suitable—even though the value of the material destroyed may be very great.

It has already been pointed out that the occult, like the "immoral woman," is constantly changing its ways. No final or exhaustive list of occult practices can ever be offered.

Over many years I have sought to help people with problems that had not been resolved by the type of counseling or ministry normally offered by the majority of churches today. So far as I could tell, these people's problems were not due to lack of sincerity or earnestness. In fact, they often seemed to be more earnest and sincere than many regular churchgoers who manifested no obvious problems.

In the cases in which I did succeed in helping such people, I almost invariably discovered some root of involvement with the occult in their backgrounds. Often they themselves did not see this as a potential cause of their problems. Yet once the occult root was exposed and dealt with, it was usually comparatively easy to resolve the other, more obvious problems.

A simple but vivid example comes to my mind. In a home prayer meeting, I found myself next to a young man in his early twenties. We had not met before, but I felt led to ask him, "Have you received the Holy Spirit?"

"Yes," he replied, but then added rather wistfully, "but I don't speak in tongues." Clearly he felt there was something lacking in his experience.

Without discussing any further the issue of tongues, I asked him, "Did you ever visit a fortune-teller?"

He reflected for a moment, and then said, "Yes, once, when I was about fifteen. But I only did it as a joke. I didn't really believe in it."

"But still," I pressed him, "you did actually have your fortune told?"

"Yes," he acknowledged rather reluctantly, and then added defensively, "but I didn't mean anything by it."

"Would you be willing to confess that as a sin," I said, "and ask God to forgive you and release you from its consequences?"

When he agreed to this, I led him in a simple prayer, in which he confessed his visit to the fortune-teller as a sin and asked God to forgive him and release him from its consequences. Then, without a further word of explanation, I put my hand on his shoulder and asked God to release the Holy Spirit within him. Instantly, without hesitation or stammering, he began to speak clearly and fluently in an unknown tongue. In a few moments he was lost in the presence of God, oblivious to all that was going on around him. The invisible barrier in his life had been removed!

Since then, I have reflected many times on my brief encounter with that young man. His problem was not lack of earnestness or sincerity. It was a failure to recognize the nature of his act in visiting the fortune-teller. He did not understand that in God's sight he had been guilty of spiritual adultery.

Suppose I had asked him, "Did you ever commit adultery with a married woman?" He would never have replied, "Yes, but I only did it as a joke. . . . I didn't mean anything by it."

Countless multitudes of people today are in a similar situation. Many of them are churchgoers. Yet, through ignorance, they have trespassed in the area of the occult and have become involved in a sin that is worse than physical adultery. Until they recognize the true nature of what they have done, they must continue under the shadow of the curse God has pronounced on all who turn away from Him to false gods. Furthermore, the same shadow may continue to rest over the lives of the next four generations of their descendants.

When confronted with these issues, Christians sometimes respond, "But I didn't know that I was doing anything wrong." My reply is to point out that in 1 Timothy 1:13–15 Paul describes himself as the chief of sinners for sins he committed "ignorantly in unbelief." Ignorance does not absolve us from the guilt of our sins, but it may dispose God to show us mercy if we repent and turn to Him.

All of us, without exception, need to consider carefully how these principles may apply in our lives. In the first two of the Ten Commandments God has pronounced His judgment on two specific sins: turning to any false god besides the one true God; and making and worshiping any artificial representation of God. These two sins include the whole area of the occult. God's judgment on those who commit them, as we have seen, extends to the four generations following.

Conversely, any one of the four generations preceding us, by having committed these sins, could be the cause of a curse over us in our generation. Each of us has two parents, four grandparents, eight great-grandparents and sixteen great-great-grandparents. This makes a total of thirty persons, any one of whom might be the cause of a curse over our lives. How many of us would be in a position to guarantee that none of our thirty immediate ancestors was ever involved in any form of idolatry or the occult?

Thank God He has provided a way of release from any curse that might have come from this source! Thank God we can avail ourselves of His provision! In the final day of reckoning, God will not hold against us the fact that our ancestors brought a curse upon us, but He will hold us guilty if we refuse to avail ourselves of the provision He has made for us to be released from such a curse.

Questions for the Study ――――――――――――――

1. According to Proverbs 26:2, behind every curse that comes on us is a *cause* .

2. True or false: Once we know the cause of a curse, we are still not able to remove it. **F**

3. The form of disobedience that will most surely provoke a curse from God is the breaking of the *first* *two* of the Ten Commandments.

4. True or false: It is enough to acknowledge the Lord as the first or greatest of all the gods. **F** *He's the ONLY God*

5. The second sin is making any artificial representation of God and offering *worship* to it.

6. In the breaking of these commandments, the curse continues for how many generations? *at least 4*

7. The word *occult* is derived from a Latin word meaning *hidden* or *covered* *over*

8. True or false: Two of the strongest cravings of human nature are the desire for knowledge and for love. **F** *knowledge & power*

9. The Bible describes turning to false gods as *spiritual adultery* and describes it as an even greater sin than *physical adultery*

10. What are the three main branches of the occult? *Divination* is the knowledge branch, *sorcery* operates through material objects and *witchcraft is the* power branch.

11. True or false: If one commits a sin not knowing it was a sin, God will not hold that person accountable. **F**

Life Application ――――――――――――――

1. Have you or anyone in your family worshiped idols or false gods? If yes, list the names of the false gods.

2. Read the lists of the different forms of the occult on pages 78–79. Have you ever participated in any of these? If yes, write down the ones you have been involved with.

Memory Verse

Like a flitting sparrow, like a flying swallow, so a curse without cause shall not alight.

Proverbs 26:2

Faith Response

Lord, I declare that You are the only true God. There is no other god besides You. You are my source for wisdom and strength.

Answers

1. Cause.
2. False.
3. First two.
4. False. He is the *only* true God.
5. Worship.
6. Four.
7. Hidden, covered over.
8. False. For knowledge and for power.
9. Spiritual adultery, physical adultery.
10. Divination (knowledge), sorcery (material objects), witchcraft (power).
11. False. Read 1 Timothy 1:13–15.

7

Various Moral and Ethical Sins

The primary form of disobedience that provokes God's curse is stated in Exodus 20:3–5: acknowledging and worshiping false gods. In addition, the Old Testament also reveals a large number of secondary forms of disobedience upon which God has pronounced a curse. In this category, in Deuteronomy 27:15–26, Moses lists twelve moral and ethical sins, all of which provoke God's curse.

Earlier in this chapter Moses had instructed Israel to carry out a solemn ceremony after they had entered the land of Canaan. On the two adjoining mountains of Ebal and Gerizim they were to offer sacrifices and set up large stones with all the words of the Law written on them. With these words in plain view, half of the tribes would first invoke a blessing on all Israelites who were obedient. Then the other six tribes would invoke a curse on all who were disobedient. To both the blessing and the curse, all the people were required to respond, "Amen!"[1]

In this way, God ordained that Israel's occupation of Canaan would confront them with two diametrically opposite alternatives: a blessing for obedience or a curse for disobedience. Between these two was no middle ground. No other option was open to them. From then onward, every Israelite who entered Canaan would either enjoy God's blessing or endure His curse.

These two alternatives are presented with stark clarity in the history of Israel, and subsequent records confirm their outworking. Nevertheless, these alternatives are not confined to Israel. They apply equally to all who would enter into a covenant relationship with God. Under the New Covenant, just as under the Old, God offers the same two alternatives: either blessing for obedience or curse for disobedience. One great delusion among Christians, which Satan carefully fosters, is that there is some third possibility, which is neither obedience, with its blessings, nor disobedience, with its curses. Neither the Old Testament nor the New offers any such option.

The twelve curses pronounced on the Israelites from Mount Ebal were detailed and specific. The following is a suggested summary of the main kinds of conduct covered by them:

Acknowledging and worshiping false gods.
Disrespect for parents.
All forms of oppressions and injustice, especially when directed against the weak and the helpless.
All forms of illicit or unnatural sex.

The final curse covered all forms of disobedience to the Law.

As always, the primary cause of God's curse is any form of involvement with false gods. This is followed by disrespect for parents. The requirement to respect our parents is restated and reemphasized in the New Testament. In Ephesians 6:1–3 Paul reaffirms the fifth of the Ten Commandments:

Children, obey your parents in the Lord, for this is right. "Honor your father and mother," which is the first commandment with promise: "that it may be well with you and you may live long on the earth."

Countless people today—including many Christians—are unaware that disrespect for parents brings God's curse. I could not estimate the number of people I have dealt with personally on this issue. Thank God that I have seen a wonderful change for the better in the lives of those who have recognized this sin, repented of it and changed their attitude toward their parents!

On this theme, it is appropriate to quote a passage from my book on marriage, *God Is a Matchmaker*.

Paul points out that the preceding four commandments had no promise attached to the keeping of them. But to this fifth commandment, relating to parents, God added a special promise: "That it may go well with you." At the same time, the promise implies a condition: If you want it to go well with you, you must be careful to honor your parents. Conversely, if you do not honor your parents, you cannot expect it to go well with you.

Bear in mind that it is possible to honor your parents without agreeing with them on all points or endorsing everything they do. You may disagree strongly with them in some matters, yet maintain a respectful attitude toward them. To honor your parents in this way is also to honor God Himself, who gave this commandment.

I am convinced that a proper attitude toward parents is an essential requirement for God's blessing on any person's life. In all the years I have dealt with Christians in teaching, pastoring, counseling, and other relationships, I have never met one who had a wrong attitude toward his parents and enjoyed the blessing of God. Such a person may be zealous in many areas of the Christian life, active in the church, energetic in ministry. He may have a place in heaven waiting for him. Yet there is always something lacking in his life: the blessing and favor of God.

I have seen many Christians, on the other hand, whose lives were revolutionized when they acknowledged a wrong attitude toward parents, repented of it and made the necessary changes. I remember one man who was convicted of a lifetime of bitterness and hatred toward his father. Although his father was already dead, this man journeyed hundreds of miles to the cemetery where his father was buried. Kneeling beside the grave, he poured out his heart to God in deep contrition and repentance. He did not rise from his knees until he knew his sin was forgiven and he was released from its evil effects. From that point on, the whole course of his life changed from frustration and defeat *Dave !* to victory and fulfillment.

The next form of conduct in the list of Deuteronomy 27 is oppression and injustice, especially against the weak and the helpless. There are certainly many examples of such behavior in our contemporary culture, but none is more likely to provoke God's curse than the deliberate aborting *G.* of an unborn infant. Who is more helpless and incapable of self-defense than a baby in its mother's womb, if its own parents do not protect it?

How strange that people who are active in the fight against racial prejudice and injustice—and rightly so—actually condone and promote the practice of abortion! Strange, too, that people who would never think of raising a hand in violence against a small child feel no compassion toward an even smaller child in its mother's womb. Somehow the substitution of the word *fetus* for *infant* dulls people's consciences. Yet the change in terminology in no way affects the real nature of such an act.

Someone has asked, "What hope is left for a society in which mothers kill their own babies?" God's attitude toward abortion is not affected by a change in terminology. He classifies it quite simply as "murder"—and deals with it accordingly. In nation after nation around the world today, millions of lives are being blighted by the curse that follows this act.

The final form of curse-provoking conduct in the list taken from Deuteronomy 27 is the abuse and perversion of the sexual relationship. Some Christians, unfortunately, have formed the impression that sex is somehow unclean, something that cannot be avoided but nevertheless needs an apology. Yet the biblical picture is just the opposite. Sex is part of the Creator's original plan for man, something sacred and beautiful. For this reason God has set stringent boundaries around the sexual act, to protect it from abuse and perversion. These boundaries are marked out by the curses pronounced in verses 20 through 23 of Deuteronomy 27.

The forbidden facts here listed cover sex with various persons related either by blood or marriage, and any form of sex with animals. The acts forbidden in the Bible also include all expressions of homosexuality. In Leviticus 18:22 God declares: "You shall not lie with a male as with a woman. It is an abomination"—also translated "detestable." This is the same word used in Deuteronomy 18:12 to describe various forms of occult practice.

Today many of these boundaries designed to protect the sanctity of sex are being deliberately set aside—sometimes even in the name of Christianity. Yet no arguments based on "situation ethics" or "the new morality" (which is by no means new) can affect or change the laws of God that govern human behavior. All who indulge in sexual perversion expose themselves to the curse of God.

It is significant that this list of acts that provoke God's curse in Deuteronomy 27 is followed immediately in Deuteronomy 28 by the complete list of blessings for obedience and curses for disobedience. It is as if God says: "Before you decide whether to obey or not, you had better give careful consideration to the consequences. So here they are!"

Questions for the Study

1. In Deuteronomy 27:15–26, Moses lists twelve _moral_
   _____ and _ethical_ sins that will provoke a curse
   from God.
2. True or false: The condition for blessings and
   curses is different under the New Testament than it
   is under the Old Testament. _F_
3. "Honor your mother and father" is the first commandment with a _promise_
4. True or false: You can have a wrong attitude toward your parents and still enjoy the blessings of
   God. _F_
5. Another form of misconduct is _oppression_ and _injustice_
   _____, especially against the weak and helpless.
6. True or false: Because we live in a modern society,
   we are no longer under the laws that govern sexual
   immorality. _F_

Life Application

1. Have you ever disrespected your parents? If so, acknowledge this sin to God and ask for forgiveness.
2. Have you ever taken advantage of the weak and
   helpless? If so, acknowledge the specific situation
   before God, ask Him to forgive you and then speak
   a word of blessing over the one(s) you took advantage of.
3. Have you ever participated in any illicit sexual relationships? If so, repent of these relationships and
   ask God to forgive and cleanse you.
4. Have you ever been on the receiving end of oppression and injustice or disrespect by your children or
   others?

Memory Verse ————————————————

Flee also youthful lusts; but pursue righteousness, faith, love, peace with those who call on the Lord out of a pure heart.

2 Timothy 2:22

Faith Response ————————————————

Lord, I will not compromise what Your Word says is truth nor will I justify my wrongdoing. I desire to walk in righteousness.

Answers

1. Moral and ethical.
2. False; it is the same. Obedience brings blessings and disobedience brings curses.
3. Promise.
4. False.
5. Oppression, injustice.
6. False.

8

Anti-Semitism

About four thousand years ago God made a choice that has affected all subsequent history. He was looking for a man who would meet His conditions so that he might ultimately become a channel of God's blessing to all nations. The man He chose was called Abram (later renamed Abraham).

God's purpose in choosing Abraham is unfolded in Genesis 12:2–3. Characteristically, blessing and curse are closely connected. God pronounces four promises of blessing upon Abraham:

"I will bless you."
"You shall be a blessing."
"I will bless those who bless you."
"In you all the families of the earth shall be blessed."

Interposed in the midst of these blessings, however, is a curse.

"I will curse him who curses[1] you."

The addition of this curse serves an important practical purpose. Any person on whom God pronounces His blessing is thereby automatically exposed to the hatred and opposition of the great enemy of God and His people: Satan. Paradoxical as it may seem, the blessing of God provokes the curse of Satan, channeled through the lips of those whom Satan controls. For this reason, when God blessed Abraham, He added His curse on all who would curse Abraham. This meant that no one could curse Abraham without incurring the curse of God in return.

In Genesis 27:29, when Isaac blessed his son Jacob, he also extended to him the same protection that God originally provided for Abraham: "Cursed be everyone who curses you." Later, under divine compulsion, Balaam uttered a prophetic revelation of Israel's destiny, which was exactly opposite to his original intention to curse Israel. Part of this revelation, recorded in Numbers 24:9, echoed the words already spoken concerning Abraham and Jacob: "Blessed is he who blesses you, and cursed is he who curses you."

Taken together, these Scriptures make it clear that both the blessing and the curse originally pronounced on Abraham were extended to his descendants, Isaac and Jacob, and then on to their succeeding generations, who are today known collectively as the Jewish people.

God did not make it impossible for His enemies to curse Abraham, Isaac, Jacob and their descendants, but He did ensure that no one could do it with impunity. From that time onward, no one has ever cursed the Jewish people without bringing upon himself a far more fearful curse: that of almighty God. In contemporary speech, the attitude that provokes this curse of God is summed up in a single word: anti-Semitism.

It would take a full-length book to trace the outworking of this curse in the history of individuals and nations from the time of the patriarchs until our day. Suffice it to say that in nearly four thousand years, no individual and no nation has ever cursed the Jewish people without bringing upon themselves in return the blighting curse of God.

The story of Nabil Haddad provides a vivid contemporary illustration of both aspects of God's promise to Abraham: on the one hand, the curse on those who revile the Jewish people; and on the other hand, the blessing that results from blessing them. Nabil is a Palestinian Arab, born in Haifa into a well-known Arab family. Subsequently, he immigrated to the United States, where he became a successful businessman. He also had a powerful personal encounter with the Lord Jesus Christ. Here is his story in his own words:

My name is Nabil Haddad. I am a Palestinian Arab born in Haifa in 1938 to Christian Arab parents.

I remember that from my earliest childhood, I would always go to bed depressed. I became determined to find a way to be happy. I knew my parents loved me, but that didn't change my unhappiness. I became convinced that if I could become rich and successful, then I would be happy. That became my goal.

In 1948, the fighting between the Arabs and the Jews began. Our whole family moved to Lebanon. In the late 1950s I came to the United States for college.

So, in America, I set out to achieve my goal of becoming rich and successful through education and business. Over the next few years, I married, became an American citizen, started a family and became a franchisee of McDonald's restaurants. By the age of thirty I was a millionaire. However, the depression had not left me. I started seeking material things—cars, trips, recreation, anything that money can buy—to make me happy. Nothing worked.

Finally, I began to ask questions: Who is this Man Jesus? Who is this One that people still talk about 2,000 years after His death? Who is this One that some people even worship?

I opened the Bible, wanting to see what this Jesus had said about Himself, and a Presence filled the room. Somehow I knew that Jesus is the Son of God. I spent most of the next year reading the Bible and talking to my friends about Jesus. But still I was depressed. During this time, I sold my nine McDonald's restaurants for a few million and started a new business. Things started to go sour. I became more depressed. I began to question God again.

"Why, Lord? Before I knew that Jesus is Your Son, I was doing fine. Now everything is going wrong!"

God replied, *What have you done with the revelation that Jesus is My Son? Nothing in your life has changed. Even Satan knows that Jesus is My Son.*

"What do You want me to do, Lord?"

Repent, and receive Him into your life.

I found someone who could show me how to pray. I repented and asked Jesus into my heart. A few months later, I was baptized in the Holy Spirit. Now I had the answer. *I no longer went to bed depressed.* But my life was still not right. My business continued to go downhill. Again I confronted the Lord.

"Lord!" I said. "You tricked me. Before I knew anything about Your Son Jesus, I was doing all right. Then you showed me He is Your Son, and things started going wrong. Then I received Him into my life, and now I'm losing everything!"

I'm a jealous God, He replied. *Your business is your god, your Rolls Royce is your god, your position is your god. I'm going to take all these false gods away from you to show you who the true living God is. But—I will restore you.*

Within ten months, I was bankrupt.

A little later I went to Fort Lauderdale for a seminar called "Curses: Cause and Cure" taught by Derek Prince. I learned that many areas of my life were under a curse—financial, physical, not enjoying my children, etc. I remembered the same kinds of problems in my father's life and in the lives of other family members.

On the third day, when Derek led the few hundred people in a prayer to be set free from curses, I stood up. People in front of me, next to me, and behind me had physical manifestations of release. But my release did not occur at the meeting. The next day, for eight straight hours, I was being released from curses with painful vomiting of things that were attached deep inside my body. When I asked the Lord what I was being delivered from, He showed me witchcraft and many other specific problems.

For months the Lord continued to show me additional areas of curses. Each time I repented and claimed my release on the basis of Jesus becoming a curse for me.

One day as I was worshiping, I said, "How great You are! You created the universe *and everything in it!*" The Lord asked me if I really believed that. I said, "Yes, Lord."

He said, *What about the Jewish people? You still hold resentment in your heart against them.*

I remembered how my whole family had always cursed the Jews. I was trained to *hate* them from my earliest years. Now, in the presence of the Lord, I said, "I renounce any resentment in my heart toward the Jewish people. I forgive them!" Immediately something changed inside of me.

Shortly after this I saw that God in His Word had told Abraham, the father of the Jews, "I'll bless those who bless you and curse those who curse you" (see Genesis 12:3). Then I realized that my finances had not been under a blessing, but under a curse—a curse of insufficiency. I had never been able to make enough money to meet my needs. Even if I made $250,000, I would need $300,000. Later, when I made $500,000, I would need $700,000 to cover my expenses.

Since 1982, when I was released from the curse of anti-Semitism and the curse of insufficiency that went with it, my income has always exceeded my expenses and my needs. And I am able to *give liberally* to the work of the Kingdom of God.

God has also healed my body and my emotions. I am totally free from depression. I can truly say I am walking in victory. My testimony has helped many others to be delivered from the curse and to live under God's blessing.

The lesson of Nabil's life is clear: *No one can afford to hate or curse the Jewish people*. This lesson was never more needed than it is today. Both socially and politically, anti-

Semitism is one of the most powerful forces at work in our contemporary world. Yet ultimately it spells disaster for all who allow themselves to be controlled by it.

Unfortunately, throughout many centuries, the professing Christian Church has often been guilty of propagating flagrant anti-Semitism. Yet the Church owes every spiritual blessing she claims to those who have been her victims: the Jewish people. Without the Jews, the Church would have had no apostles, no Bible and no Savior.

Here is one main reason for the present lukewarm, powerless condition of so much of Christendom—especially in Europe and the Middle East, where anti-Semitism is most deeply entrenched. The story of Nabil Haddad points to the solution: open acknowledgment of anti-Semitism as a sin, followed by repentance and renunciation. This will result in a deep, inner change of heart toward the Jewish people, and a recognition of the measureless spiritual blessings the Christian Church has received through them.

On this basis, we can then entreat God to remove the dark shadow of the curse, which at present rests upon major sections of the Church, and to replace it with His blessing.

Questions for the Study ────────────────

1. In Genesis 12:2–3, how many promises of blessing did God pronounce on Abraham? *4*
2. True or false: God provided protection for Abraham from Satan by interposing a curse in the middle of the blessings. *True. I will curse him who curses you.*
3. The Scriptures make it clear that the blessings and the curse originally announced to Abraham have been passed down to the *Jewish* people.
4. True or false: No one has ever cursed Abraham, Isaac, Jacob or their descendants without bringing on himself a more fearful curse. *T*
5. Both socially and politically, *anti-Semitism* is one of the most powerful forces at work in our contemporary culture.
6. True or false: The Christian Church over the centuries has protected the Jewish people. *F*
7. To break the curse of anti-Semitism, one must acknowledge it as a *sin*, and follow that with *repentance* and *renunciation*

Life Application ────────────────

1. What did you learn about anti-Semitism that you did not know before?
2. Has this chapter changed how you think about Israel and the Jews? In what way?
3. Have you ever cursed Israel or the Jews? If so, take a few moments to repent and ask God to forgive you.

Memory Verse ────────────────

Pray for the peace of Jerusalem: "May they prosper who love you."

Psalm 122:6

Faith Response

Lord, I bless Israel in Your name and I speak a word of peace to Jerusalem.

Answers

1. Four.
2. True. "I will curse him who curses you."
3. Jewish.
4. True.
5. Anti-Semitism.
6. False. The Church has often propagated anti-Semitism.
7. Sin, repentance, renunciation.

9

Legalism, Carnality, Apostasy

In Jeremiah 17:5 God pronounces His curse on another kind of sin, which, like anti-Semitism, is at work in many sections of the Church: "Thus says the LORD: 'Cursed is the man who trusts in man and makes flesh his strength, whose heart departs from the LORD.'"

In this context—as in many other passages of Scripture—the word *flesh* does not denote the physical body. Rather, it denotes the nature each of us has received by inheritance from our common ancestor, Adam. Adam did not beget any children until he himself had transgressed God's commandment. The essential motivation of his transgression was not so much the desire to do evil as it was the desire to be independent of God.

This desire is at work in every one of Adam's descendants. It is the distinctive mark of the "flesh." In the field of religion, it seeks to perform righteous acts without depending on the supernatural grace of God. No matter how good its intentions, the final product will always be an "Ishmael," not an "Isaac."

The adjective that Scripture applies regularly to the flesh is *corrupt*. Although it can produce much that is designed to impress the mind and the senses, it is all tainted by corruption. The outcome of all its efforts is described in Hebrews 6:1 as "dead works," from which God requires us to repent.

The kind of person described in Jeremiah 17:5 is not a stranger to God's grace. This is indicated by the closing phrase: "whose heart departs from the LORD." If he had never known the Lord, he could not be said to "depart" from Him. A person of this kind has experienced God's supernatural grace and power, but then turns back to relying on his own natural ability. His conduct reveals that he has more confidence in what he can do for himself than in what God can do for him. He has, in fact, "snubbed" God. It is this attitude that calls forth God's curse.

The next verse describes the outworking of the curse that such a person brings upon himself: "For he shall be like a shrub in the desert, and shall not see when good comes, but shall inhabit the parched places in the wilderness, in a salt land which is not inhabited."

What a vivid picture of a person under God's curse! He finds himself living in "parched places" and "a salt land." All that surrounds him is barren and dreary. Refreshing may come to others all around him, but in some mysterious way it always passes him by. He is doomed to barrenness and frustration.

The curse of Jeremiah 17:5–6 is at work in the lives of many individuals, but it also applies to a much wider area. It is one real but invisible cause of the barrenness and ineffectiveness of many sections of the contemporary Christian Church. Almost every movement of any significance in Christendom can trace its origin to a powerful, supernatural work of God's grace and God's Spirit. It is to this, above all else, that these movements owe the impact they have made on history.

Yet, today, many—perhaps most—of these movements no longer place much emphasis on the grace of God and the power of the Holy Spirit. They have turned back to relying on the best that they can accomplish by their own efforts. They are "trusting in man"—that is, in themselves—and "making flesh their strength." Surely, but imperceptibly, "their heart has departed from the LORD." They have, perhaps, achieved religious and intellectual "respectability," but in so doing they have forfeited God's favor. In its place, they have brought upon themselves the dark shadow of the curse pronounced in Jeremiah 17:5.

To put human ability in the place of divine grace is to exalt the carnal above the spiritual. The effect will be manifested in many different areas. For example:

Theology will be exalted above *revelation*;
intellectual education above *character building*;
psychology above *discernment*;
program above *the leading of the Holy Spirit*;
eloquence above *supernatural power*;
reasoning above *the walk of faith*;
laws above *love*.

All these errors are different manifestations of one great, basic error: putting man in a place God has reserved solely for the Lord Jesus Christ.

This was the kind of situation Paul sought to deal with in the churches of Galatia. In Galatians 3:1–10 he traces the problem from its source to its culmination. The following is a brief outline.

In verse 1 Paul identifies the source as a deceiving satanic influence that he calls *witchcraft*: "O foolish Galatians! Who has *bewitched* you . . . before whose eyes Jesus Christ was clearly portrayed . . . as crucified?"

An alternative version renders Paul's question, "Who has put you under a *spell*?"

This satanic influence had obscured the only source of God's all-sufficient grace: *Jesus Christ crucified*. Cut off in this way from God's grace, His people inevitably turn back to the only alternative: a system of religious laws. This leads to Paul's next question in verse 2: "Did you receive the Spirit *by the works of the law*, or by the hearing of faith?" (emphasis added). The word normally used to describe this is *legalism*. Since this word is often used in an imprecise way, however, it is important to define it more exactly.

Legalism may be defined in two related ways. First, it is the attempt to achieve righteousness with God by observing a set of rules.

In Romans 3:20 Paul has ruled this out with absolute finality: "Therefore by the deeds of the law no flesh will be justified in His sight, for by the law is the knowledge of sin." The word *the* in front of *law* is put in by the translator. What Paul actually says is, "*By the deeds of law* no flesh will be justified." The primary reference is to the Law of Moses, but the statement applies no less to any other set of religious rules. Law can show us that we are sinners, but it does not have the power to change us.

Alternatively, *legalism* could be defined as the attempt to impose any extra condition for achieving righteousness beyond what God Himself has laid down. God's requirement is stated in Romans 4:24–25:

> It [righteousness] shall be imputed to us who believe in Him who raised up Jesus our Lord from the dead, who was delivered up because of our offenses, and was raised because of our justification [in order that we may be reckoned righteous by God].

This is God's simple but all-sufficient requirement to attain righteousness: that we entrust ourselves to Him, believing that He did two things on our behalf. First, He delivered Jesus to death for our sins. Second, He raised Jesus from the dead that we might be reckoned righteous. God asks no more than this, and no one has ever been authorized to add anything to God's requirements.

After that, once we have received righteousness in this way by faith, the righteous acts that are appropriate will flow out of our faith. But if we add any extra requirement for attaining righteousness, God will not meet us on this basis, and the righteous acts will not follow. We will never be able to go beyond the best that we can achieve by our own fleshly efforts.

This explains Paul's next question in Galatians 3:3: "Having begun in the Spirit, are you now being made perfect *by the flesh*?" (emphasis added). The normal term for this is *carnality*—that is, relying on our own fleshly nature. Further on, in Galatians 5:19–21, Paul lists at least fifteen "works of the flesh." Not one of them is good or acceptable to God, because the flesh is not capable of producing anything that God will accept. In Romans 8:8 Paul sums this up: "So then, those who are in the flesh *cannot* please God" (emphasis added).

Finally, in Galatians 3:10, Paul states the culmination of this descending process: *a curse*. "For as many as are of the works of the law are under the curse."

Thus, by the logic of the Holy Spirit, Paul analyzes the problem of the Galatian churches, which is also the problem of many contemporary churches. It stems from a deceiving, satanic influence that infiltrates the church and diverts the attention of God's people from the only source of His grace: *Jesus Christ crucified*. Paul categorizes this influence as *witchcraft* or *a spell*.

Cut off in this way from the source of grace, Christians inevitably degenerate into carnality and legalism. The final outcome of this downward drift is *a curse*. It has already been pointed out—in chapter 6—that spells and curses are the main tools of witchcraft.

In this way, the truth of Jeremiah 17:5–6 is carried over into the New Testament and finds its expression in Galatians 3:1–10. Trusting in the works of the law (legalism) and making flesh our strength (carnality) culminate in a curse. As a result, God's people find themselves living in "parched places" and "a salt land."

Carnality can take many forms. Often these are obvious and unappealing to people with a religious outlook. Some typical examples would be: sexual uncleanness or immorality; vulgar language; overindulgence in food or drink; driving personal ambition; uncontrolled anger or other evil passions. What makes legalism especially dangerous is that it appeals to earnest, dedicated men and women who would not easily be entrapped by these more obvious sins of the flesh. Yet in its final consequences, legalism is just as deadly as other, less "respectable" sins. It is Satan's favorite tool to divert Christians who could otherwise become a serious threat to his kingdom.

For me personally, the analysis of the Galatian problem is no mere exercise in abstract theology. On the contrary, it is very real, and also painful. In 1970, in Fort Lauderdale, I found myself sovereignly and supernaturally "joined" to a small group of ministers from various backgrounds. None of us had anticipated what happened to us, and none of us understood what God had in mind for us. Doubtless, if we had continued to rely on the Holy Spirit who had initiated our relationship, He would have gradually unfolded His purpose to us, but that was not the path we followed.

All too soon, and without our discerning what was happening, the various features of the Galatians 3 "syndrome" began to manifest themselves. Our decisions and actions were no longer initiated by the Holy Spirit, but were based on an elaborate system of rules and concepts that had been devised. We continued to acknowledge the Holy Spirit, but in the way that guests in a restaurant might acknowledge a waiter. If we felt we needed something, we would summon

Him briefly. But for the most part we relied on methods and plans of our own devising.

Looking back, I realize now that the work the Holy Spirit had initiated among us posed a serious threat to Satan. He resorted, consequently, to the tactics that had been so successful in Galatia, and in countless other situations throughout subsequent Church history. There were two decisive steps. First, he displaced the cross from the center of our lives and ministries. Second, he displaced Jesus as "head over all things" in our practices and relationships.[1] By an inevitable process, we degenerated into the normal type of religious organization, operating on the plane of our natural reason and ability.

Paradoxically, one main cause of our problems was the very fact that we had had a supernatural beginning. Like the Galatians, we had "begun in the Spirit." From that beginning, there was no easy or painless route by which we could simply become just another religious organization, functioning on the natural plane and taking our place alongside countless similar groups throughout Christendom. As Paul pointed out to the Galatians, that which has been initiated by the Holy Spirit can never be brought to completion by human flesh.

It was not long before we were confronted by the outworking of the curse we had thus brought on ourselves. Its manifestations were characteristic of other similar developments throughout Church history. Personal relationships were ruptured; congregations were split and scattered; promising ministers were cut short or else diverted from God's purpose; once-enthusiastic Christians were blighted by frustration and disillusionment. Many abandoned their faith. If we had been obliged to give a name to it all, we would have had to call it "Ichabod, saying, 'The glory has departed'" (1 Samuel 4:21).

The product of all religious activity that is not initiated and directed by the Holy Spirit is summed up, in Hebrews 6:1, by the phrase *dead works*. For this, the remedy is stated in the same verse: *repentance*. This was made real to me personally. I could not blame others. I had to accept responsibility for what I had been involved in. More than anything else, I realized that I had grieved and slighted the Holy Spirit.

I saw that I had to confess my sins to God and trust Him for forgiveness and restoration. This was a personal decision that only I could make. I could not make it on behalf of others, but if I could find a path that led to restoration, then those who saw their need could follow the same path. In 1983 I repented and made the break.

In His mercy, God showed me, step by step, the path I was seeking. I discovered that there is a way to pass out from under the curse and enter once more into the blessing. If I had not made this discovery, this book would never have been written. For those who may find themselves in a similar situation, I offer a full explanation of the steps they need to take in Section 3: "From Curse to Blessing."

In Galatians 1:6–9 Paul exposes another way a curse may come upon the people of God: *apostasy.*

> I marvel that you are turning away so soon from Him who called you in the grace of Christ, to a different gospel, which is not another; but there are some who trouble you and want to pervert the gospel of Christ. But even if we, or an angel from heaven, preach any other gospel to you than what we have preached to you, let him be accursed. As we have said before, so now I say again, if anyone preaches any other gospel to you than what you have received, let him be accursed.

The kind of person here described is one who represents himself as a minister of Christ, but perverts the central truth of the Gospel. Paul declares that such a person brings a curse upon himself. The Greek word translated "accursed" is *anathema.* It denotes something that provokes

God's wrath and is subject to His irrevocable condemnation and rejection.

The Gospel contains a central core of revealed truth that has been accepted and upheld by the general Church throughout all generations. It may be summed up as follows:

> Jesus Christ is the divine, eternal Son of God, who became a member of the human race by virgin birth. He led a sinless life, died on the cross as a propitiatory sacrifice for the sins of humanity, was buried and rose again in bodily form from the grave on the third day. He ascended into heaven, whence He will return to earth in person, to judge the living and the dead.
>
> Everyone who repents of sin and trusts in the sacrifice of Jesus receives forgiveness of sins and the gift of eternal life.

It is important to emphasize that the Gospel centers in the death and resurrection of Jesus. In 1 Corinthians 15:3–4 Paul sums up its message in three historical facts: "Christ died for our sins according to the Scriptures. . . . He was buried . . . He rose again the third day according to the Scriptures."

The first authority that Paul cites in support of these facts is "the Scriptures"—at that time meaning the Scriptures of the Old Testament. As further confirmation of the resurrection, Paul goes on to list various eyewitnesses who saw Jesus after He rose from the dead. Their testimony is secondary, however, to that of the Old Testament Scriptures.

In two successive statements, Paul then stresses that faith in the bodily resurrection of Jesus is essential to salvation: "And if Christ is not risen, then our preaching is empty and your faith is also empty. . . . And if Christ is not risen, your faith is futile; you are still in your sins!" (1 Corinthians 15:14, 17).

In 2 Thessalonians 2:3 Paul warns that at the close of this age there will be widespread apostasy from the Christian faith. There are strong reasons for believing that we are now in the predicted period of apostasy. In some major Christian denominations, many recognized leaders have publicly renounced faith in the Scriptures and—in particular—in the bodily resurrection of Christ. Probably they do not realize that their declaration of unbelief is in itself a fulfillment of the Scriptures they are rejecting!

One fact, however, they cannot change: Unless they repent, those who in this way pervert the Gospel bring upon themselves the wrath and the curse of God.

Questions for the Study

1. What is the adjective that Scripture applies regularly to the flesh? _corrupt_
2. True or false: The kind of person described in Jeremiah 17:5–6 is a stranger to God's grace. _F_ — _has experienced a then turned his back on God's grace_
3. A person under the type of curse cited in Jeremiah 17:5–6 is under both _barrenness_ and _frustration_
4. To put human ability in the place of divine grace is to exalt the _carnal_ above the _spiritual_
5. True or false: One definition of legalism is to attempt to achieve righteousness with God by observing a set of rules. _T_
6. What are the two things we must believe in order to attain righteousness with God? _① God delivered Jesus to death for our sins ② He raised him from the dead_
7. Making flesh our strength is called what? _carnality_
8. In 2 Thessalonians 2:3 Paul warns that at the close of this age there will be widespread _apostasy_ from the Christian faith.

Life Application

1. Carnality can take many forms. Have you experienced the carnal man exerting itself over the spiritual man? How? _compulsive overeating_
2. In Galatians 3:1–10 Paul describes people who begin in the Spirit but end up in the flesh. What did you learn about how this happens?
3. Have you ever fallen prey to legalism? If so, how?
4. Hebrews 6:1 calls all activity that is not directed by the Holy Spirit "dead works." Have you ever participated in dead works? The remedy given is repentance. Spend a few moments with the Lord and ask Him to reveal any dead works in your life, and then voice a prayer of repentance and ask for His forgiveness.

Memory Verse ——————————————————————

Christ has redeemed us from the curse of the law.

Galatians 3:13

Faith Response ——————————————————————

Jesus, my desire is to walk in the Spirit and not in the flesh. I will keep my eyes on You and Your grace.

Answers

1. Corrupt.
2. False. This person has experienced God's grace and power but has turned his back on God to rely on his own ability.
3. Barrenness, frustration.
4. Carnal, spiritual.
5. True.
6. That the Father delivered Jesus to death for our sins and that Jesus was raised from the dead.
7. Carnality.
8. Apostasy or falling away.

10

Theft, Perjury, Robbing God

The last three prophets of the Old Testament—Haggai, Zechariah and Malachi—all deal with various areas in which Israel experienced the outworking of God's curse. It is as though these prophets were given the task of summarizing the history of the Israelites since they had come under the Law of Moses, and of confronting them with the reasons why specific curses of the Law had come upon them.

In Zechariah 5:1–4 the prophet describes a vision he had of God's curse coming upon the homes of His people:

I looked again—and there before me was a flying scroll!

He asked me, "What do you see?"

I answered, "I see a flying scroll, thirty feet long and fifteen feet wide."

And he said to me, "This is the curse that is going out over the whole land; for according to what it says on one side, every thief will be banished, and according to what it says on the other, everyone who swears falsely will be banished. The LORD Almighty declares, 'I will send it out, and it will enter the house of the thief and the house of him who swears falsely by my name. It will remain in his house and destroy it, both its timbers and its stones.'"

NIV

The curse that Zechariah depicts enters the house of all who have committed two specific sins: theft and swearing falsely. (The contemporary term for the latter is *perjury*.) Having once entered, the curse remains until it has destroyed the entire house—timbers and stones and all.

This is a vivid picture of the way a curse works, if we once admit it into our lives. We cannot set limits of our own choosing to the areas that will be affected by it. Unless we repent and seek God's mercy to deliver us, it will ultimately destroy the whole house.

The prevalence of these two sins of theft and perjury in our contemporary culture may be measured by some simple statistics. Theft is so pervasive today in the United States that nearly 10 percent of the price of goods displayed in retail stores is due to the cost of insurance against theft. Here is a little-publicized cause of inflation! On the other side, perjury defrauds the U.S. Internal Revenue Service of billions of dollars each year through dishonest tax returns. Complete honesty in this area could perhaps wipe out the entire budget deficit!

According to Zechariah's vision, the curse that follows these two sins of theft and perjury affects not merely the individual, but also his entire house. In biblical Hebrew, the word *house* applies not simply to a material structure, but also to the people who live in it—that is, a family. Much more than would at first appear, these two sins, and the curse that follows them, have contributed to the breakdown of family life, which is a unique feature of our present age. Their ultimate effect will be similar to that of the scroll Zechariah saw in his vision: the erosion of whole nations and even an entire civilization.

Earlier, Haggai had given an equally vivid
blight that was affecting the lives of his peo

> "Is it time for you yourselves to dwell in your paneled house,
> and this temple to lie in ruins?" Now therefore, thus says
> the LORD of hosts: "Consider your ways!
>   "You have sown much, and bring in little; you eat, but
> do not have enough; you drink, but you are not filled with
> drink; you clothe yourselves, but no one is warm; and he who
> earns wages, earns wages to put into a bag with holes."
>
> Haggai 1:4–6

The curse Haggai describes can be summed up in one
word: *insufficiency*. To all outward appearances, the Israelites had everything they required to satisfy their main
material needs. Yet for some reason they could not understand, there was always a deficiency. God had to send them
a prophet to show them that the invisible force eroding their
provisions was a curse they had brought upon themselves
by putting their own selfish concerns before the needs of
God's house.

Many of the affluent nations of the world today face a
similar situation. Most people are earning far more than
their parents or grandparents ever earned. Yet while the
previous generations enjoyed a sense of contentment and
security, the present generation is plagued with a restless
craving that is never satisfied. In some of these nations,
the level of personal indebtedness is higher than it has
ever been.

Malachi, the last of the three prophets, combines the
charges already brought against Israel by his two predeces-
sors. He accuses his people not only of a wrong attitude
toward God, but also of theft in its most serious form:
robbing not merely men, but even God Himself.

> "Will a man rob God? Yet you have robbed Me! But you say,
> 'In what way have we robbed You?' In tithes and offerings.

115

You are cursed with a curse, for you have robbed Me, even this whole nation."

Malachi 3:8–9

This passage reveals a principle that governs God's dealings in every age and dispensation: He keeps a record of what His people offer to Him. More than a thousand years earlier, God had ordained that Israel should set aside for Him the first tenth of her total income, in cash or in kind. This was one important mark of her covenant relationship with God. Disobedience in this was a breach of her covenant.

Now, through Malachi, God presents His account. In respect of all that His people have unlawfully withheld, He charges them with "robbery." He points out that this has brought a blighting curse on the whole nation and on every area of their lives.

But God does not end on this negative note. In the next verse He instructs His people how to pass out from under the curse and enter into His blessing:

> "Bring all the tithes into the storehouse, that there may be food in My house, and try Me now in this," says the LORD of hosts, "If I will not open for you the windows of heaven and pour out for you such blessing that there will not be room enough to receive it."

Malachi 3:10

To pass from the curse to the blessing, God requires from His people two things: repentance and restitution. In every case of robbery, these requirements never vary, whether it is God or man who has been robbed.

In the New Testament, God never establishes a specific law, like that of the Old Testament, requiring Christians to set aside for Him a tenth of their total income. The covenant of grace does not operate through laws enforced from

116

without, but through laws written by the Holy Spirit in the hearts of believers. In 2 Corinthians 9:7 Paul instructs Christians, "So let each one give *as he purposes in his heart*, not grudgingly or of necessity" (emphasis added).

One thing, however, is certain: The Holy Spirit will never cause a believer to be stingy. In Psalm 51:12 David prays to the Lord, "Uphold me by Your *generous* Spirit" (emphasis added). One distinctive characteristic of the Holy Spirit is generosity. God Himself is the greatest of all givers. When His Spirit moves on the hearts of His people, He will make them like Himself: generous givers.

In Hebrews 8:6 the writer contrasts the Old and the New Covenants, and reminds Christians that they have entered into "a better covenant, which was established on better promises." It is inconceivable that people who enjoy this better covenant should be less generous in giving to God than those who were under an inferior covenant. If God's people under the Law gave Him their tithes—and much more—how could Christians under grace possibly justify doing less? The standards of grace are higher, not lower, than those of law.

Throughout all dispensations, one basic principle continues unchanged: Stinginess toward God provokes His curse, but liberality releases His blessing.

Questions for the Study

1. The last three prophets of the Old Testament all deal with various areas in which Israel experienced the outworking of God's curse. Who are these prophets? *Zechariah, Haggai, Malacchi*

2. In Zechariah 5:1–4 what two specific sins caused the curse to enter all the houses of those who committed them? *theft, perjury*

3. Malachi 3:8–9 describes what sin that brings a curse? *robbing God*

4. In Haggai 1:4–6 what one word describes this curse? *insufficiency*

5. To pass from the curse to the blessing, God requires two things from His people: *repentance* and *restitution*

6. Stinginess toward God provokes His curse while *generosity* releases His blessing.

Life Application

1. Have you committed any of the three sins discussed in this chapter?
2. Have you seen evidence of the curse in your life?
3. To pass from the curse to the blessing requires repentance and restitution. Go before the Lord and repent for your participation in these sins and then ask God what He would have you do by way of restitution.

Memory Verse

Let each one give as he purposes in his heart, not grudgingly or of necessity; for God loves a cheerful giver.

2 Corinthians 9:7

Faith Response

Lord, all that I have is Yours. I commit myself to "walk in the way of goodness, and keep to the paths of righteousness" (Proverbs 2:20).

Answers

1. Haggai, Zechariah, Malachi.
2. Theft and perjury.
3. Robbing God.
4. Insufficiency.
5. Repentance, restitution.
6. Liberality.

11

Authority Figures

Both blessings and curses are part of a vast, invisible spiritual realm, which affects the lives of every one of us. One central and decisive factor in this realm is *authority*. Without a grasp of the principles of authority, it is impossible to understand the realm of the spirit or to function effectively in it.

The twentieth century witnessed an almost worldwide revolt against forms of authority that have been generally recognized by the human race for millennia. Major areas of social structure that have been affected include the family, the church and the various branches of secular government.

People often assume that this revolt has changed or abolished these forms of authority, but *this is not so*. The principles that govern the exercise of authority are as objective and universal as the law of gravity.

A person in an attitude of revolt may decide to reject the law of gravity and to jump out of a window on the tenth floor. But his rejection of that law in no way changes or invalidates it. He will still fall to his death on the sidewalk below. The same applies to the laws that govern the exercise of authority. People may ignore them or reject them, but the course of their lives will still be determined by them, whether they recognize it or not.

Throughout the universe there is one, and only one, supreme source of authority: God the Creator. God does not normally exercise His authority directly, however, but delegates it to others of His choice. After Jesus rose from the dead, He told His disciples, "All authority has been given to Me in heaven and on earth" (Matthew 28:18). Since that time, God has placed all authority in the hand of Jesus. But Jesus, in His turn, delegates to others the authority He has received from the Father.

Thus authority throughout the universe may be pictured as an extremely strong cable, descending from God the Father to Jesus. In the hand of Jesus, the cable is separated into countless smaller cables that reach to persons whom He has appointed—both angelic and human—in various parts of the universe.

One term used in the Bible to denote a person who exercises authority is *head*. In 1 Corinthians 11:3, for instance, Paul writes: "But I want you to know that the head of every man is Christ, the head of woman is man, and the head of Christ is God."

By this analogy of headship, Paul depicts a "cable" of authority that originates with God the Father, descends to Christ and from Christ to the man who fills the role of husband and father in a family. By virtue of this relationship, the man is the appointed authority in his home.

In human social relationships, the husband/father is the primary example of a person appointed to exercise authority. There are, however, many other commonly recognized authority figures: a ruler over his people; a military commander over his soldiers; a teacher over his pupils; a pastor over the members of his congregation.

God alone has *absolute* authority. All other forms of authority are subject to limitations of various kinds. Delegated authority is valid only *within a given sphere*. A ruler's authority, for instance, is normally limited by the laws of his nation and does not extend to "private" areas in the lives of his subjects. A father's authority over his family does not permit him to infringe upon the laws of the secular government. A teacher has authority over his pupils only within the limits of school life. A pastor has authority over his congregation only in matters that are governed by the form of religion the congregation has accepted.

All the above examples are generalities. For complete accuracy, it would be necessary to add many other qualifications and restrictions. Also, there could be cases where two forms of authority overlap, giving rise to conflicts. The examples given are sufficient, however, to establish the basic principles that govern the exercise of authority.

It is commonly assumed that whenever authority is abused, it is automatically canceled. This may happen in extreme cases, but normally it is not so. Authority in some form is a basic necessity for any kind of social life. Authority that is abused may inflict many hardships, but even so it is better than the alternative, which is anarchy.[1]

In many population centers today, the air that people breathe has become so polluted that it is dangerous to health. God does not for this reason, however, remove all air from that area of the earth's surface. Even polluted air is preferable to no air at all. Similarly, even abused authority is better than anarchy.

One important way a person may exercise authority is by blessing those under his authority. Genesis 27 records the tremendous importance that both Jacob and Esau attached to the blessing of their father, Isaac. And with good reason, since the history of their descendants has been determined ever since by the words Isaac spoke over each of them at that time. Nor is Isaac an isolated exception. On the contrary, all through the Bible, the blessing of a father is considered second in importance only to that of God Himself.

Implicit in the authority to bless, however, is the authority also to curse. Blessing and cursing can never be separated from one another, any more than heat from cold or day from night. This means that persons with authority may exercise it in one of two ways: to bless or to curse. The same authority that makes a blessing effective makes a curse equally effective.

One dramatic example is provided by the family life of Jacob. Genesis 31 records how Jacob, with his two wives, two concubines and eleven children, departed by stealth from his Uncle Laban in Mesopotamia and set out to return to the land of Canaan. Laban, however, with a company of his relatives, set out in pursuit of Jacob and overtook him in the mountains of Gilead. There followed a confrontation between them, in which Laban accused Jacob of stealing his *teraphim* (household images or "gods" used for divination and supposed to "protect" a home from evil forces).

What Jacob did not know was that Rachel, the wife he loved most dearly, had secretly taken the images. Consequently, Jacob reacted indignantly to Laban's accusation. He challenged Laban to search all his family's belongings, and then—to protest his innocence—he added what was in effect a curse: "If you find anyone who has your gods, he shall not live" (Genesis 31:32, NIV).

Laban did proceed to search all the belongings of Jacob's household, but Rachel succeeded in keeping the *teraphim* hidden. Nevertheless, the words of Jacob's curse were charged with a husband's authority. They were equivalent to a sentence of death on the person who had stolen the images. The fact that Jacob did not realize that his words were directed against Rachel did not prevent the curse from taking effect. Shortly afterward, in giving birth to her second son, Rachel died in labor (see Genesis 35:16–19). Such is the authority of a husband, either to bless or to curse!

It should be added that, by taking possession of false "gods," Rachel had trespassed in the area of idolatry and of the occult. Thus, by her own action she had already forfeited God's protection and exposed herself to the curse that inevitably follows occult involvement. Here is a clear example that the laws governing blessings and curses are—in their own sphere—as real and as objective as the law of gravity. They work, whether people recognize them or not.

In God's plan for marriage, husband and wife become "one flesh," thus merging their separate identities in a new unity. On this basis, a husband naturally includes his wife in the authority they share jointly over their children. Failing to do this, the husband may become arbitrary or despotic.

Today, however, it is more common for a husband to go to the opposite extreme by reneging on his responsibilities to his wife and children, and even abandoning them completely. In such circumstances, the wife is left to carry on her own a burden that should have been shared by the two of them together. The result is frequently a complete breakdown of the whole family structure. All credit should be given to Christian wives who find themselves in this situation, but by faith, prayer and the grace of God successfully carry the extra burden that has been thrust upon them.

In the case of Jacob, he did not realize that the words he had uttered were directed against Rachel. In our contemporary culture, however, it often happens that a husband knowingly and deliberately directs bitter and crushing words against his wife. Here is a typical example:

Mary, who never received any domestic training from her mother at home, marries Jack, a business executive with a quick temper. Mary never succeeds in serving meals that are tasty or attractive. For a while, Jack exercises self-control and contains his impatience. Finally, he blurts out his frustration: "I'm sick of the way you serve our meals. You'll never learn to cook!" He repeats this—with variations—on many subsequent occasions.

From then on, Mary's hands tremble whenever she brings food to the table. Meals become an ordeal from which she longs to escape. After some years, the marriage breaks up. But the curse pronounced by Jack follows Mary through the rest of her life. Although talented and successful in other areas, she never does learn to cook. Whenever she finds herself in a kitchen, something dark comes over her that inhibits her natural ability. There is only one solution for her: to recognize the fact that her husband put a curse on her and to seek the release God has provided.

It also transpires, however, that Jack has pronounced a curse on himself, without knowing it. From the time he said, "I'm *sick* of the way you serve our meals," he begins to develop chronic indigestion, for which physicians can find no natural cause or cure. Just like Mary's inability to cook, Jack's indigestion follows him to the end of his days.

(Chapter 12 will cover this important area of *self-imposed* curses.)

Obviously there could be many variations to the story of Jack and Mary. Mary's problem might be overweight. Jack's comment would take this form: "You just don't have the willpower that it takes to lose weight. You'll be fat for the rest of your life."

Or again, Mary might be one of those women who do not know how to handle money. Her budgeted amount runs out before the week is up. She never succeeds in balancing her checkbook. Jack might give vent to his frustration by saying: "A fourth-grader could handle money better than you do. You don't deserve to prosper. You'll be struggling for the rest of your life."

Picture another couple: Jim and Jane. Jim's language is more brutal than Jack's. He frequently closes bitter arguments by saying, "I hate your guts!" In the years that follow the inevitable divorce, Jane requires surgery in the area of the abdomen for three successive conditions, none of them directly related to the others.

The correct diagnosis for all three of Jane's problems is stated in Proverbs 12:18: "There is one who speaks like the piercings of a sword." It required the surgeon's scalpel to deal with the invisible wounds that Jim had inflicted by his bitter words.

Words such as Jack uses against Mary—or Jim against Jane—proceed out of moods that may range from impatience to anger to rage. Usually there is demonic pressure behind them. They are like barbed arrows, tipped with poison. Once they penetrate the flesh, the barbs make it difficult to pull them out. Yet if they are left in, the poison spreads on the inside.

Greater even than the authority of a man over his wife is that of a father over his children. This is the most basic of all authority relationships. It is actually an extension of the eternal relationship of Father to Son within the Godhead.

Just as a father's blessing has measureless potential for good, so a father's curse has a corresponding potential for evil. Sometimes such a curse may be uttered deliberately. More often, perhaps—as in the relationship of a husband to his wife—a father may speak words to a child that are not deliberately intended as a curse, but nevertheless have exactly the same effect. Each of the following examples is a composite of elements I have encountered in real-life situations.

A father has three sons. The firstborn is welcome just because he is that—the firstborn. The youngest has unusual talent and an outgoing personality. But the middle son has neither of these factors in his favor. He broods over misunderstandings, but tends to keep his feelings to himself. Furthermore, the father sees in this middle son aspects of his own character that he does not like, but has never been willing to deal with in his own life. He finds it less painful to condemn them in his son than in himself.

As a result, the middle son never has a sense of his father's approval. In the end, he no longer tries to win it. His father interprets this as stubbornness. More and more frequently, he vents his disapproval in words such as: "You don't even try!" "You're lazy!" "You'll never make good!" Little does he realize that he is pronouncing an evil destiny that may easily follow his son through the rest of his life.

I could not count the men I have encountered personally whose lives have been blighted by negative, critical, destructive words spoken by a father. Out of these encounters I have learned that such words are, in reality, a *curse*. The passage of time does not diminish their effect. Men past middle age may still find their lives blighted by words a father spoke to them in childhood. The only effective solution is to deal with them specifically as a curse, and to apply the remedy God has provided.

As with the cases of Jack and Mary, or Jim and Jane, there are many different variations to such a situation. A father who is skillful with his hands, for example, may have a son who is unusually late in developing manual dexterity. After the son has bungled various practical tasks assigned to him, the father exclaims, "Your fingers are all thumbs!" or, "You have two left hands!"

The father may speak these words jokingly, not in anger. Nevertheless, they make a permanent impact on the son. Thirty years later he is still embarrassed or diffident every time he is confronted with even a simple practical task. This continues to be an area of his life in which he never succeeds. Yet his root problem may not be so much lack of skill as lack of confidence. He has never rebuilt the confidence his father unintentionally destroyed in childhood.

Daughters, too, like sons, may suffer from the effects of a father's negative words. A teenage daughter, for instance, acutely conscious of her acne, spends hours each morning in front of her mirror, struggling to cover the blotches with various types of skin cream. Her father, waiting to drive her to school, is increasingly irritated by her failure to be ready on time. One day, when the daughter is later than usual, his irritation explodes. "You're wasting your time in front of that mirror!" he barks. "You'll never get rid of your pimples!" Twenty years later the daughter—now a married woman with children of her own—is still struggling vainly to cover up her acne.

Bitter, angry words—whether spoken by a husband to his wife or a father to his child—are usually the outcome of a period of growing inner tension. It is like a whistling kettle placed on a stove to boil. At first, the tension builds up inwardly, without any outward indication, but when the water inside reaches the boiling point, the steam is expelled and the whistle is blown. After that, there is no way to recall that whistle. The only remedy is to take the kettle off and cool the water down.

For a Christian, this means turning to God with an urgent, inward prayer: *Lord, I'm beginning to lose control, but I yield my spirit to You. Will You please take control?*

Otherwise, when irritation and anger continually build up inside a person, they will ultimately be expelled, like steam, in hurtful, wounding words. The curse that accompanies them is like the whistle. Once it has been uttered, there is no way to recall it. Then the only solution is to recognize that a curse has been uttered, and seek God's help to revoke it.

A mother, too, has authority over her children, which is either shared with her husband or delegated by him. Sometimes, however, a mother is not content with the exercise of her legitimate authority. Instead, she exploits her children's affection and loyalty to gain illegitimate control over them and to direct the course of their lives. Another example of "witchcraft"! This becomes particularly evident when her children come to choose their mate. If the mother approves of their choice, she is all sweetness. But if she disapproves, a totally different side of her character appears.

In the section that follows, a husband and wife each relate their experiences resulting from a curse pronounced by the wife's mother at the time of their marriage. They describe, first of all, the effects that the curse had on each of them; then how they became aware of the curse and took the scriptural steps to be released from it.

Husband

Living under a curse is like living in a vapor. The effects can be seen, yet it is without clear form and substance. Even though you may experience success, you feel only *frustration* and *hopelessness*.

For me, the blessings of God always seemed somewhat remote and unattainable. I often knew the Lord's presence and moved in the spiritual gifts, yet satisfaction in ministry and life always seemed just out of reach. My wife and children had nagging health problems, and finances were continually short (even though we tithed, gave regularly and lived frugally).

Though I knew clearly the ministry to which God had called me, I could not move into it. Most of my work seemed to end with just a measure of fruitfulness. I could start things, but couldn't complete them. I seemed to be facing some kind of invisible resistance.

This struggle went on for years. Then one day I found myself explaining the situation to a group of fellow ministers, including Derek Prince. They discerned a curse coming on my family from my mother-in-law. I will let my wife explain.

Wife

Early in my marriage I spent two days in prayer and fasting. I felt the Lord show me that there was a curse in my family. My husband and I were newly baptized in the Holy Spirit and had never even heard of such a thing as a curse. Our experience, as we have sought to become free, could be compared to peeling layers off an onion.

This curse revolves around a spirit of witchcraft that has operated through the women in my family, especially my mother. My family was churchgoing, moral and quite "normal," but the witchcraft worked subtly to undermine the authority of the men in our family, while manipulating the other family members.

I was not aware of the extent of my mother's control until I became engaged. As my loyalty began to switch to my future husband, I could sense her growing resentment. That was when my mother said, "He'll never make any money and you'll have to work the rest of your life." All through the years of our marriage I have labored against that "curse." I was determined to "show her" by not working in an outside job, but I was, in fact, controlled by it because I wasn't free to have a job! Also, my husband and I could never visualize ourselves as prosperous, and we have had continual financial problems.

Then, shortly after I married, my mother said, "You know you're not a strong person physically." I felt as if someone had hit me on the head! What she said was such a shock to me because I had never perceived myself as a weak or sickly person. On the contrary, I had always been healthy and athletic. So I began to think that perhaps I had been wrong, and really wasn't strong physically. . . . Subsequently I have battled a lot of physical ailments, some of long duration.

I also struggled because I was responding to my own husband and children in some of the same ways my mother did. This left me with a sense of hopelessness. How could I get completely free from this curse? Witchcraft had exercised control in several generations of my family. It seemed the spirit associated with it truly believed it had the right to dominate me and, in fact, it believed it *owned* me!

Whenever I would be ministered to for deliverance, this spirit would whisper to me that I couldn't really be completely free. I blamed my mother. . . . Through a slow, "layer-by-layer" process of revelation and deliverance I came to see that my enemy is *not* my mother. I have forgiven her, and acknowledged the curse of witchcraft that had been influencing both of us.

Since having ministry specifically to break these curses, I have had to learn to battle old thought and habit patterns. Now I daily confess with confidence: "Through the sacrificial offering of Christ on the cross I have been purchased out from under the curse and have entered into the blessings of Abraham, whom God blessed in all things" (see Galatians 3:13–14). *Christ has redeemed me from the curse!*

Husband

After prayer for breaking of curses, there was a distinct "clearing of the air." The changes have been neither dramatic nor immediate, but they have been real. There is a sense of *direction* in my life.

There is *progress*. I feel that I have a scriptural degree of control over my life and that I can take my rightful place in my family. I can also see productivity and fruitfulness as a result of my labors.

Most important to me, there is *hope*. The nebulous darkness of the future has been replaced by excitement and joy at what God is doing. The "fog" is clearing!

It is important to see that the wife's mother was not aware of all the effects her words had on her daughter and son-in-law. She herself was the prisoner of a spiritual force that came from her own family background. Quite possibly it had affected that family for many generations. The mercy of God provided a way of release from its control.

School life is another area in which authority relationships are important, although the authority of a teacher over pupils is not so clear-cut as that of a parent. Negative words spoken by a teacher to a pupil may have the same blighting effect as if they had been spoken by a parent. For instance, a teacher may become exasperated by a pupil who is inattentive and slow to learn, and blurt out words such as: "You'll never be able to read properly!" or "You always get things the wrong way 'round; you'll never succeed!"

In all probability, the teacher is unaware of the danger of such words and will never see the result they produce on the pupils in later life. Yet I have met grown men and women who have been struggling for most of their lives against the effect of words spoken by a teacher in grade school. I recall one dedicated Christian lady who had been haunted for forty years by a sense of inferiority going back to a remark by a teacher who had told her, "You're shallow!" In fact, it would have been difficult to find anyone to whom these words were less applicable.

Examples have been given above of the potentially blighting effect of words spoken by people who have authority proceeding out of a relationship. The specific relationships—chosen merely as examples—were those of a husband, a father, a mother and a schoolteacher. There is one characteristic thread that runs through the various ways in which these authority figures expressed themselves. It can be summed up in one brief phrase: "You'll never prosper—or succeed!"

Surely it is significant that Moses, in describing to Israel the outworking of "the curse of the law," used precisely the same words: "You shall not prosper in your ways" (Deuteronomy 28:29). For my part, whenever I hear a person using such words, I am always on my guard against the possibility that a curse is being uttered.

Religion is another main area in which authority is vested in people who hold certain offices. Consequently, their words have a potential for good or evil that corresponds to the authority of their office. For many centuries in Europe, one main weapon used by the popes of the Roman Catholic Church was their papal "ban" (that is, *curse*), which they would proclaim on all whom they deemed to be heretics. It would be impossible to write an accurate history of Europe without taking into account the effects of this papal ban. Even rulers of nations feared it more than an actual declaration of war.

In the Protestant section of the Church, no person has ever achieved an authority equal to that of the pope. Nevertheless, wherever there is ecclesiastical authority, there is always the possibility of its misuse. Even the pastor of a small "independent" church, with a mere handful of members, can speak words that are, in effect, a curse.

I am reminded of a man with excellent business qualifications—let's call him Frank—who came for counseling. He had spent ten frustrating years in which nothing went right for him and he was barely able to support his wife and family. I asked Frank if anything had happened in his life at the point when things began to go wrong for him. His mind went back to a period when he and his family had been attending a small independent church. After various disagreements with the pastor, they had withdrawn their membership.

Since the family was one main source of the church's income, the pastor reacted out of fear and insecurity. The final exchange between Frank and the pastor was acrimonious—on both sides. Finally the pastor closed by saying: "God put you in this church. If you leave, you'll be out of His will. Nothing will ever go right for you!"

Sure enough, from that time on, nothing did go right for Frank. Fortunately, when he understood the cause of his frustrations, he was able to release himself from that pastoral curse. But first he had to forgive the pastor and put things right between them. After that, the course of Frank's life changed for the better.

Frank's case is not exceptional. I have met an astonishing number of people who have been through similar experiences. Almost invariably, the pastor has taken the same line: "God put you in this congregation. If you leave, you'll never prosper!" (Note those familiar words!) But thank God, He has provided a solution—for both parties to the dispute.

In 1985, while ministering in Australia, I was confronted by the effects of an ecclesiastical curse that had persisted for more than three centuries. A lady—whom we will call Margaret—heard me teach on the theme of blessings and curses. At the end of my message, recognizing clear evidence of a curse at work in her family, Margaret stood—with many others—and repeated the prayer of release. Later, she sent me a letter giving the background of her case.

Her ancestors were from Scotland, from a clan called Nyxon. In the 1600s this clan had been involved in border wars between the Scots and the English. As a result, the Bishop of Scotland (who was appointed by the English) had pronounced a curse on the entire Nyxon clan. Margaret enclosed a copy of the curse, which decreed—among other things—that the members of the clan should be hanged, drawn and quartered,[2] and their entrails fed to the dogs and the swine. After the clan had been defeated in battle, this sentence was duly carried out on those members who were captured alive.

Two years later, on my return to Australia, I met Margaret briefly. Later she wrote this letter:

> Thank you so very much for praying for me and my family, and for delivering God's prophetic words to us while here in Melbourne. You asked if our family had changed since the release from the curse. I did not have time to tell you when we spoke, but, yes, my whole family—my husband, my two daughters, ages 24 and 23, and my son, age 21—have all come to know the Lord over the last two years and now we have joined a Full Gospel church here in Melbourne.

What astonishing testimony to the power of a curse! It had followed Margaret's clan through three centuries, and Margaret's branch of the clan right across the world, from Britain to Australia. Once the curse had been identified and revoked, the invisible barrier that kept God's blessing from Margaret's family was removed, and her entire household entered into salvation.

This naturally raised the question, How many other families are being kept from salvation because of an unrecognized curse?

Questions for the Study

1. It is impossible to understand the realm of the spirit or to function in it without a grasp of the *principles of authority*

2. God alone has *ultimate* authority.

3. All through the Bible the blessing of the *Father* is considered second in importance only to that of God Himself.

4. True or false: The same authority that makes a blessing effective makes a curse equally effective. *T*

5. What is the most basic of all human authority relationships? *Father over his children*

6. True or false: Once a curse has been uttered, there are several ways to recall it. *F: no way to recall a curse*

7. The one characteristic thread coming from an authority figure curse is that the other person will never *succeed* or *prosper.*

Life Application

1. Have you ever been in a place of authority over people? If so, do you recall speaking evil or negative words? Take a few moments and ask God to forgive you and then speak a word of blessing over those people's lives.

2. Do you relate to any of the stories in this chapter? In what way?

3. Do you see any situations or conditions in your life that may be the result of someone in authority over your life who spoke a curse? What specifically?

Memory Verse

Yes, my inmost being will rejoice when your lips speak right things.

Proverbs 23:16

Faith Response

Heavenly Father, I will endeavor always to speak with grace, to speak words of life and not death, blessings and not curses.

Answers

1. Principles of authority.
2. Absolute.
3. Father.
4. True.
5. That of a father over his children.
6. False. There is no way to recall it. One must seek God's help to revoke it.
7. Prosper, succeed.

12

Self-Imposed Curses

In one of the examples from the previous chapters, Jack said to his wife, *"I'm sick* of the way you serve our meals." By these words he unwittingly brought upon himself a curse of indigestion that continued to afflict him for the rest of his life.

With this example in mind, it is time now to examine more thoroughly this whole area of *self-imposed curses*. It is of vital importance for all who are concerned about their own personal welfare. It uniquely exposes the frightening power of the words we speak about ourselves. They are frequently like boomerangs, which come flying back to strike the one who spoke them.

In Matthew 12:36–37 Jesus gives a solemn warning about the danger of words carelessly spoken:

> "But I say to you that for every idle word men may speak, they will give account of it in the day of judgment. For by your words you will be justified, and by your words you will be condemned."

Jesus here focuses on "idle words"—that is, words spoken carelessly, without premeditation. Often when a person says something foolish or negative about himself, he then excuses himself by saying, "But I didn't really mean it." Yet it is precisely against words of this kind, which people "don't really mean," that Jesus warns us. The fact that the speaker "doesn't really mean them" does not in any way minimize or cancel the effect of his words. Nor does it release him from his accountability.

In Proverbs 6:2 Solomon warns a person who has unwisely put up security for a neighbor: "You have been trapped by what you said, ensnared by the words of your mouth" (NIV). This is only one of countless ways in which people are "ensnared by the words of their mouths." We may easily be caught in a snare of this kind without realizing it, but to get free demands the conscious application of biblical principles. We need to remember that God takes our words seriously, even when we ourselves do not.

Mark 14:66–72 records how, in the court of the high priest, Peter three times denied that he was a disciple of Jesus. To enforce his third denial, he actually "began to curse and swear." In other words, he invoked a curse on himself.

Peter was quickly stricken with remorse, but it is doubtful even so that he understood the full implication of his own words. Three days later, at the empty tomb, the angels told the women, "Go, tell His disciples—*and Peter*—that He is going before you into Galilee" (Mark 16:7, emphasis added). Peter was no longer reckoned as being one of the disciples. By his own words he had forfeited his standing as a disciple of Jesus.

Later, John 21:15–17 records how, by the Sea of Galilee, Jesus graciously opened the way for Peter to regain his standing as a disciple. He asked Peter three times, "Do you love Me?" Peter answered each time in the affirmative, but he was grieved that Jesus put the question three times. He did not realize that Jesus was leading him in this way to revoke his previous denials. For each time that he had made a wrong confession, he now made the right confession. On this basis, he was reinstated as a disciple.

The way Jesus dealt with Peter established a pattern for all who need to be released from the snare of a bad confession. There are three successive steps: Repent—Revoke—Replace. First, we must acknowledge that we have made a wrong confession and *repent* of it. Second, we must *revoke* it—that is, we must unsay, or cancel, whatever we said that was wrong. Third, we must *replace* our previous wrong confession with the right one. These three steps, taken in faith, can release us from the snare.

Genesis 27:12–13 provides another example of a self-imposed curse. Rebekah was persuading her son Jacob to deceive Isaac, his father, now blind, in order to obtain his blessing (which Isaac intended to pronounce on his other son, Esau). Jacob was eager for the blessing, but fearful of the consequences if Isaac should discover his deception.

"Perhaps my father will feel me," he said, "and I shall seem to be a deceiver to him; and I shall bring a curse on myself and not a blessing."

Rebekah responded immediately, "Let your curse be on me, my son."

Rebekah's plan to obtain the blessing for Jacob succeeded, but her own words exposed her to a curse that kept her from enjoying the fruits of her success. Her mood quickly became one of pessimism and cynicism. Soon afterward we find her saying to Isaac, "I am weary of my life because of the daughters of Heth; if Jacob takes a wife of the daughters of Heth . . . what good will my life be to me?" (Genesis 27:46).

Almost immediately, too, Jacob had to leave home to escape the vengeance of his brother, Esau, and he was gone for about twenty years. The Bible tells us nothing about the rest of Rebekah's life or about the time and manner of her death. It would seem, however, that she never had the satisfaction of seeing Jacob enjoying the blessing that her deceptive scheme had obtained for him.

Over the years I have heard many people speak about themselves in the same way as Rebekah: "I'm tired of living. . . . Nothing ever goes right. . . . What's the use? . . . I give up! . . . I might as well be dead. . . ." I have learned by experience that expressions such as these almost always indicate a self-imposed curse at work in the life of the one who utters them.

A much more tragic and far-reaching example of a self-imposed curse is depicted in Matthew 27:20–26. Against his own judgment, the Roman governor, Pilate, consents to release to the crowd a murderer named Barabbas and to impose the death sentence on Jesus instead. In order to disassociate himself from this act, however, Pilate washes his hands in front of the crowd and says, "I am innocent of the blood of this just Person."

To this the crowd responds, "His blood be on us and on our children."

These words combined two forms of curse: a *self-imposed* curse on themselves; a *relational* curse on their descendants. The objective record of history confirms the outworking of both. Within one generation the Roman armies had destroyed Jerusalem, and either killed or sold into slavery the entire population.

Since that time, for nineteen centuries, a dark strand of bloodshed and tragedy has been interwoven in the destiny of the Jewish people. Time after time, in pogrom after pogrom, Gentile rulers have turned loose against defenseless Jews violent, depraved men of the caliber of Barabbas—the one whom they had chosen.

But thank God, that is not the end! God has provided a way of reconciliation and restoration. Through His unsearchable wisdom and His marvelous mercy, the death of the One who was executed as a criminal has provided a way of escape from the consequences of the curse. Chapter 17 will explain this in detail.

Earlier, in chapter 8, we saw that when God originally called Abraham and blessed him, He also pronounced a curse on all who would curse him. Later, this curse was reaffirmed when Isaac blessed Jacob, and once more when Balaam pronounced a prophetic blessing on Israel as a nation. In this way God provided protection for Jacob and his descendants—the Jewish people—from all who would seek to put a curse on them. Subsequent history revealed, however, that there was one kind of curse from which even God could not protect His people: *the curse they pronounced on themselves*.

The same applies to Gentile Christians who have become heirs to Abraham's blessing through the New Covenant initiated by Jesus. Included in the provisions of the Covenant is the right to invoke God's protection against curses that proceed from any external source. But there is one kind of curse against which even God cannot provide protection: *the curses that Christians pronounce upon themselves*.

This is one way in which Christians frequently bring upon themselves various kinds of trouble of which they do not understand the source. By speaking negative words about themselves, they shut themselves off from blessings and expose themselves to curses.

In this, too, the history of Israel provides a vivid example. Chapters 13 and 14 of Numbers record how Moses sent twelve tribal leaders to spy out the land of Canaan, which God had promised to Israel as an inheritance. Two of them—Joshua and Caleb—returned with a positive report: "Let us go up at once and take possession, for we are well able to overcome it" (Numbers 13:30). The other ten gave a negative report that focused on giants and walled cities. Their conclusion was: "We are not able to go up against the people, for they are stronger than we" (Numbers 13:31).

In due course, the Lord pronounced His judgment. To all those Israelites who gave credence to the negative report He

141

said: "Just as you have spoken in My hearing, so I will do to you: The carcasses of you who have complained against Me shall fall in this wilderness" (Numbers 14:28–29). The carcasses of the unbelieving spies were the first to fall. To Joshua and Caleb, on the other hand, the Lord promised that they would take possession of the land concerning which they had given a positive report.

All those spies—both the believing and the unbelieving—determined their own destiny by the words they spoke concerning themselves. Those who said, "We are able to enter the land," did enter it. Those who said, "We are not able," did not enter. God took them at their own word. He has not changed! To Christians, just as much as to Israelites, God still says, "Just as you have spoken in My hearing, so I will do to you."

Earlier, in chapter 5, we listed seven characteristic conditions that may be marks of a curse. Often it is the way in which people speak about themselves that exposes them to these conditions. Without recognizing it, such people are actually pronouncing curses upon themselves. To guard against this, they need to recognize the wrong forms of speech that they have been using and to cultivate new, positive speech patterns in their place.

The list below repeats the seven conditions that may indicate a curse, but adds under each heading typical forms of speech that commonly open people up to the condition described. These few examples should be sufficient to indicate the kinds of expressions that are dangerous and the areas in which it may be necessary to change. For our part, Ruth and I have learned to exercise continual vigilance and self-control in the way we speak about ourselves.

1. Mental and/or emotional breakdown

"It's driving me crazy!"

"I just can't take any more."

"It makes me mad to think. . . ."

142

2. Repeated or chronic sicknesses (especially if hereditary)

"Whenever there's a bug, I catch it."

"I'm sick and tired. . . ."

"It runs in the family, so I guess I'm the next."

3. Barrenness, a tendency to miscarry or related female problems

"I don't think I'll ever get pregnant!"

"I've got the 'curse' again."

"I just know I'm going to lose this one—I always do!"

4. Breakdown of marriage and family alienation

"The palm reader said my husband would leave me."

"Somehow I always knew my husband would find another woman."

"In our family we have always fought like cats and dogs."

5. Continuing financial insufficiency

"I never can make ends meet—my father was the same."

"I can't afford to tithe."

"I hate those 'fat cats' who get all they ever want—it never happens to me!"

6. Being "accident-prone"

"It always happens to me!"

"I knew there was trouble ahead. . . ."

"I'm just a clumsy kind of person."

7. A history of suicides and unnatural or untimely deaths

"What's the use of living?"

"Over my dead body!"

"I'd rather die than go on the way I am."

143

People who use this negative kind of language are unconsciously inviting evil spirits to take them over. The type of evil spirit that responds is determined by the language used. There are classes of spirits that correspond to each of the seven categories listed above.

One kind of spirit that is particularly common is the spirit of "death." This responds to the kind of language listed under the category of "A history of suicides and unnatural or untimely deaths." It produces a sense that life is meaningless and hopeless, and a morbid tendency to focus on thoughts of death. It is often manifested also in a never-ending series of physical infirmities, for many of which there is no obvious medical cause.

Ultimately, this spirit of death will either drive a person to suicide or cause untimely death in some other way. In John 8:44 Jesus warned us that Satan is a murderer. One of the agents that he uses to murder people is the spirit of death, which causes people to die before their time. When I shared this with a physician friend, he confirmed that he often saw people die when there was not sufficient medical cause to explain it.

It may be that in one or another of the categories listed above you have recognized things that you yourself have said. If so, don't be discouraged! There is a way out! Earlier in this chapter the apostle Peter provided an example of the three steps that are necessary to escape from a self-imposed curse: Repent—Revoke—Replace.

First, we must recognize that we have made a negative confession about ourselves and we must *repent* of it. Second, we must *revoke* it—that is, unsay or cancel it. Third, we must *replace* our previous wrong confession with the right one. All this will be explained more fully in chapter 21.

Another way in which people can bring a curse upon themselves is by pledges or oaths that are required for admission to a closed fraternity or sorority, or to a secret society. I recall a situation in which my first wife, Lydia, and I were seeking to help a young Christian woman be set free from demonic bondage. In spite of many prayers and struggles, there was no deliverance. Suddenly Lydia was prompted to tell the young woman to take off a ring she was wearing. As soon as she did so, she was set free without further struggles.

Lydia acted solely on the prompting of the Holy Spirit. She knew nothing about the ring, which was actually a college sorority ring. To join the sorority the young woman had been required to make certain pledges that were inconsistent with her Christian faith. By discarding the ring, she effectively canceled those pledges and regained her liberty as a child of God.

On another occasion, Lydia and I were part of a group ministering to a young woman who confessed that she had been a priestess of Satan. She was wearing a ring that symbolized her "marriage" to Satan. When we told her she would have to take the ring off, she did so—but then, under the compulsion of Satan, she swallowed it. A young man present received a special anointing of faith, and commanded the woman to regurgitate the ring, which she promptly did! We then threw the ring into a nearby lake. The final stage in the woman's deliverance followed when she publicly burned all the clothes she had worn while worshiping Satan.

Incidents such as these have made very real for me the directions given in Jude 23: "Save others, snatching them out of the fire; and on some have mercy with fear, hating even the garment polluted by the flesh" (NASB).

In both the above instances, satanic bondage was associated with a ring. The significance of a ring is that it often symbolizes a covenant relationship. In our Western culture, for example, it is normal for a man and his wife each to wear a ring, symbolizing the covenant relationship of marriage. By biblical standards, a covenant is the most solemn and powerful form of relationship into which a person can enter, whether the covenant is between God and man, or between man and his fellow men. Satan is well aware of this, and he therefore exploits covenant relationships of his own making in order to gain the strongest possible control over people.

For this reason, in Exodus 23:32, God instructed the Israelites concerning the idolatrous nations of Canaan: "You shall make no covenant with them, nor with their gods." God was warning His people that if they entered into a covenant with the Canaanites who worshiped false gods, that covenant would bind them not merely to the Canaanites, but also to their gods. They would thus be bringing themselves into bondage to those gods.

One section of contemporary society to which this warning particularly applies is Freemasonry. Masons claim that the nature of their association is a secret, but this is not correct. All the major rites and formulas of Freemasonry have been publicized at various times, both by people who were formerly Masons (including some who had advanced to the highest degree) and by others who have carefully examined the material that is available to any competent researcher.

For present purposes, it is sufficient to point out two facts about Freemasonry. First, in order to be initiated, a person has to bind himself by the most cruel and barbarous oaths never to reveal any of Masonry's secrets. It would be impossible to find anywhere a more frightening example of self-imposed curses than these oaths.

Second, Masonry is a false religion. Some Masons would deny that it is a religion, but here are some of the main features that clearly mark it as such: Masonry has its own *revelation*; its own *temples*; its own *altars*; its own religious *symbols* and *emblems* (which include a *ring*); its own *confession of faith*; its own *priests*; its own *rituals*. Finally, it has its own *deity*, a false god, whom it calls a "Creative Principle" or "the Great Architect of the Universe."

Masonry is a *false religion* because it acknowledges a *false god*. Many of the objects and symbols associated with Christianity—including the Bible—are used in Masonry, but this is a deliberate deception. The god whom Masonry acknowledges is *not* the God of the Bible. Although the sacred, biblical name of four letters—JHVH (commonly spelled out as "Jehovah")—is used in Masonic literature, it is interpreted as referring to a divine entity that combines in itself both male and female principles. Again, the Royal Arch degree uses an abbreviated form of the name Jehovah in combination with abbreviated forms of two heathen deities, Baal and Osiris, and acknowledges this "combined" being as god. This is nothing short of a deliberate insult to the one true God revealed in the Bible as Jehovah.[1]

For my part, I had no interest at all in Freemasonry until I began to discover the harmful effects it had produced in the lives of people who came for prayer. Some of the most frightening examples that I have encountered of curses at work in people's lives were associated with Freemasonry. The effects were manifested in the second and third generations of those who had a Mason in their family background.

One case made a special impression on me. At the close of a Sunday morning worship service in Australia, Ruth and I were praying for people who needed healing. One of those who came forward was a young woman whose dull eyes, unkempt hair and slurred voice suggested a background in the subculture. In her arms she carried a tiny baby.

"She just won't take anything to eat," the mother mumbled with her eyes averted. "Just an ounce or two at a time."

"How old is she?" we asked.

"Six weeks," the mother replied, but the baby looked more like six days than six weeks old.

When Ruth and I placed our hands on the mother to pray for her, she fell backward under the power of the Holy Spirit. As she fell, Ruth caught the baby from her and held it in her own arms. Two church workers began to pray for the mother on the floor.

Ruth then received a word of knowledge by the Holy Spirit. "The woman's father is a Freemason," she said to the two workers. "Tell her to renounce that spirit."

The mother on the floor struggled to get out the words, "I renounce . . . that spirit . . . of Freemasonry." As soon as she uttered those words, the evil spirit came out of her with a prolonged scream. At the same moment, the baby in Ruth's arms emitted a precisely similar scream, and then became limp. The workers helped the mother onto her feet, and Ruth placed the baby back in her arms.

About six hours later we were back again in the same church for an evening service. At the close, the same young woman came up once more with her baby.

"How's she doing?" we asked.

"She's completely different," the mother replied. "She's taken three full bottles since the morning!" I could not help thinking that the mother, too, had undergone a dramatic change, which shone out of her eyes and sounded in the clarity of her voice.

I reflected later that in one brief encounter we had seen visible evidence of a curse due to Freemasonry that had carried over to at least two generations: from the father himself who was a Mason, to his daughter and then to his granddaughter, a baby six weeks old. I determined from then on that I would be diligent to warn people of the harm that Masons bring not only on themselves, but on the members of their families, even those who have no direct involvement in Freemasonry.

To all who have made a pledge or a vow binding them to an evil association, such as those mentioned above, Solomon offers an urgent word of counsel in Proverbs 6:4–5: "Give no sleep to your eyes, nor slumber to your eyelids. Deliver yourself like a gazelle from the hand of the hunter, and like a bird from the hand of the fowler."

There are two minimum requirements for deliverance. First, you must make a verbal renunciation of your association. *What you have said with your lips, only you can unsay*. It is best to do this in the presence of sympathetic witnesses who will support you with their faith.

Second, you must get rid of, and destroy, all the emblems, books and other materials that were marks of your association. In all the three types of situations mentioned above, a ring was of special significance. In the case of a Freemason, there would also be various other objects—particularly the apron. Remember the words of Jude 23: "Hating even the garment defiled by the flesh."

Questions for the Study ────────────

1. True or false: The negative or foolish words you say about yourself do not count if you do not really mean them. *F*

2. What are the three successive steps to release you from the snare of a bad confession? *Repeat* ~~Renounce~~ *Revoke* *Replace*

3. What is the one curse God cannot protect His people from? *self-inflicted curse*

4. True or false: When people use negative language over themselves, they are unconsciously inviting evil spirits to take them over. *T*

5. Another way to invoke a self-imposed curse is by taking a *pledge* or an *oath* to a fraternity, sorority or secret society.

6. What, by biblical standards, is the most solemn and powerful form of relationship into which a person can enter? *covenant*

7. True or false: Freemasonry is not a religion. *F*

8. There are two minimum requirements for deliverance from association with secret societies. What are they? *verbal renunciation* *destroy all physical links to society emblems, books etc*

Life Application ────────────

1. Are there areas of your life in which you are experiencing self-imposed curses? If yes, what specifically?

2. Repent of speaking negative words over your life. Revoke the curse and speak a word of blessing that is the opposite of the curse.

3. Have you or anyone in your family been part of a secret society or cult? Which one(s)?

4. Do you possess any articles associated with secret societies or cults? Can you get rid of them? If not, why not?

5. Take some time and assemble these articles and destroy them.

Memory Verse

I will praise You, for I am fearfully and wonderfully made.

Psalm 139:14

Faith Response

Thank You, Lord, that Your thoughts toward me are precious and that the sum of them is great! I am Your workmanship (see Psalm 139:17; Ephesians 2:10).

Answers

1. False. This does not cancel the effect of the words, nor does it release you from accountability.
2. Repent, revoke, replace.
3. The curse we pronounce on ourselves.
4. True.
5. Pledge, oath.
6. Covenant.
7. False. It has temples, altars, priests and rituals.
8. Verbal renunciation and the destruction of all emblems, books and other materials involved.

13

Servants of Satan

In this chapter we will uncover a completely different source of curses: servants of Satan.

Attitudes toward Satan among Christians vary between two extremes. Some ignore Satan totally, and try to act as if he is not real. Others are afraid of him and give him far more attention than he deserves. Between those two extremes there is a scriptural balance.

Satan is a created being, a rebellious angel, who was cast out of God's heaven. He rules over a spiritual kingdom of evil, rebellious angels, together with lesser evil spirits, who are called "demons."

The name *Satan* means "adversary" or "opposer." He is the unchanging, implacable enemy of God Himself and of the people and the purposes of God. His aim is to bring the whole human race under his control. His primary tactic is deception, of which he is a master. In Revelation 12:9 he is described as "the great dragon . . . that serpent of old, called the Devil and Satan, *who deceives the whole world*" (emphasis added).

Satan already exercises dominion over the great majority of mankind—all those who are in an attitude of rebellion against God. In Ephesians 2:2 he is described as "the spirit who now works in the sons of disobedience." Most of these in rebellion have no clear picture of their real condition. They are simply driven to and fro by forces they do not understand and cannot control.

There are those among them, however, who have deliberately opened themselves up to Satan, even though they may not be aware of his true identity. In pursuit of power and material gain, they systematically cultivate the exercise of the supernatural forces Satan has released to them. Such servants of Satan are recognized in almost all cultures and have been given a variety of different titles: witch doctor, medicine man, mchawi, shaman, tohanga, wizard, witch, priest or priestess of Satan, and so on. In almost all tribal cultures throughout the world there is a special name for this kind of person.

Jesus Himself is our main source of information concerning Satan. When He sent out seventy disciples to prepare the way before Him, they returned with joy, saying, "Lord, even the demons are subject to us in Your name." To this Jesus responded, "Behold, I give you the authority to trample on serpents and scorpions, and over all the power of the enemy, and nothing shall by any means hurt you" (see Luke 10:17–19).

Jesus did not deny that Satan was real or that he had power. But He promised His disciples that the authority He conferred upon them would make them victorious over Satan's power and would protect them against all his attempts to harm them. It is important for all of the Lord's servants to recognize the authority He has given them and to learn to exercise it effectively.

Curses are one of the main weapons that servants of Satan use against the people of God. This is vividly illustrated by the story of Balak and Balaam in Numbers 22–24.

153

Balak was king of the territory of Moab, on the east of the Jordan. On their journey from Egypt to Canaan, Israel had encamped on the border of Moab. Balak felt his kingdom was threatened, but he lacked the strength or the courage to launch an open attack on Israel. Instead, he hired Balaam to pronounce curses on them, in the hope that Israel would thus be weakened to the point where Moab could defeat them. Balaam was a "witch doctor," famous throughout the whole region, who commanded a high fee for his services.

Many Christians today would dismiss all this as superstitious "nonsense," devoid of any real power. God's reaction, however, was entirely different. He viewed the curses that Balaam might pronounce as a serious threat to Israel. Consequently, He intervened supernaturally and warned Balaam not to accept the assignment. But Balaam was eager for the wealth Balak had promised him, and so went ahead with the intention of doing what Balak had asked. In due course, however, each time Balaam tried to pronounce curses on Israel, God again intervened and changed the proposed curses into blessings!

Subsequently, in Deuteronomy 23:5, Moses reminded Israel of this incident as evidence of God's love for them: "Nevertheless the LORD your God would not listen to Balaam, but the LORD your God turned the curse into a blessing for you, because the LORD your God loves you."

One important fact needs to be emphasized: God did not view Balaam's proposed curses against Israel as empty words that had no power. He regarded them as a serious threat to Israel, and for this reason He intervened personally to frustrate Balaam's intention.

Time has not changed God's viewpoint. He does not ignore or belittle curses directed against His people by servants of Satan. On the contrary, as Jesus said, God recognizes the power of Satan, but equips His own servants with superior power.

The Bible presents various pictures of the activities of Satan's servants. These serve to warn God's servants, against whom these satanic activities are often directed. In Ezekiel 13:17–20, for example, God condemns certain false prophetesses, or sorceresses:

> "Likewise, son of man, set your face against the daughters of your people, who prophesy out of their own heart; prophesy against them, and say, 'Thus says the Lord GOD: "Woe to the women who sew magic charms on their sleeves and make veils for the heads of people of every height to hunt souls! Will you hunt the souls of My people, and keep yourselves alive? And will you profane Me among My people for handfuls of barley and for pieces of bread, killing people who should not die, and keeping people alive who should not live, by your lying to My people who listen to lies?"
>
> 'Therefore thus says the Lord GOD: "Behold, I am against your magic charms by which you hunt souls there like birds."'"

Some of the details are not clear, but it seems that these women played the typical role of a witch doctor. Anyone who had a quarrel with some other person would hire them to use their magic arts against that person. One of their methods was to attach magic charms to people's clothing. In this way, they "hunted souls" and actually killed innocent persons. In return, they were paid in handfuls of barley or pieces of bread.

This is not some far-fetched accusation reminiscent of the Middle Ages. It is a charge brought against these women by God Himself. Furthermore, servants of Satan have used similar methods for the same purposes all through the centuries and still continue to use them today.

In 1979–80, in the city of Bath in the west of England, archaeologists uncovered the remains of a temple of the goddess Minerva, dating back to the Roman period. The

155

priests in this temple had a similar ministry to that of the sorceresses in Ezekiel's day. People seeking revenge on someone would employ the priests to write out an appropriate curse against that person. The writing of the curse required special skills possessed only by the priests. Once the curse had been written, some kind of magic ceremony was used to direct it against the person who was its target. For all this, of course, the priests received appropriate payment. Also, the worshipers would cast their votive offerings for the goddess into the spring associated with the temple.

This way of using curses and magical arts is still a familiar part of daily life among the majority of the world's peoples, particularly in Asia, Africa, Oceania and Central and South America. The following account comes from a missionary friend of mine who has lived his whole life in Zambia, in central Africa, and is intimately acquainted with the languages and the customs of the people there.

> At a General Conference of Christians in our rural district of Zambia, the Holy Spirit had spoken a strong prophetic word calling for holiness in the Church. Many Christians were convicted of sin in their lives and had truly repented, confessing their sin and pleading for God's forgiveness.
>
> After the service, an elder from one of our remote village churches came to the preacher in tears, trembling all over, confessing to the terrible sin of *murder through witchcraft*.
>
> The elder told him that for some years he had been fighting with his fellow elder in the church who was senior to him. The situation had gotten so bad that he had decided to punish him by going to a local witch doctor and paying him to curse this other elder. The witch doctor had been happy to do so, especially as he knew that these men were supposed to be Christians. He asked for a large down payment, and then told the man to come back the following day.

156

When he returned, the elder found the witch doctor sitting under a tree with a mirror in his hand and a bowl of witchcraft medicine on the ground before him. The witch doctor then proceeded to sponge the medicine all over the mirror, and asked the elder to look carefully at the mirror and tell him what he could see.

Startled, the elder saw the face of his fellow elder quite clearly. Whereupon the witch doctor took a razor blade and cut across the throat of the face reflected in the mirror. Immediately the mirror was covered in blood.

The elder cried out, "You have killed him! I only asked you to curse him." The witch doctor replied with a chuckle, "I thought I would do the job properly whilst I was at it!"

The elder hurried home. To his horror he learned that his fellow elder was indeed dead, having died mysteriously of a sudden hemorrhage. The elder was terrified of the consequences of his action, so he had kept quiet about it. Now the Holy Spirit had powerfully convicted him of his sin.

Fortunately for him, "where sin abounded, grace did much more abound." Through confession, repentance and faith in Jesus Christ, the man was not only brought to forgiveness and peace with God, but to the reality of the new birth.

Some Western readers might be disposed to dismiss all of this as primitive, superstitious practices from "darkest Africa." But the truth is that even in the more highly civilized nations (so-called), occult practices, which had been on the decline, are once again making tremendous inroads. In West Germany, for example, many businessmen, who would never seek counsel from a Christian minister, make a regular practice of consulting a fortune-teller concerning their business deals.

In the mid-1980s a leader of the Satanic Church in America was interviewed on television. He was asked if it is true that Satanists practice human sacrifice. He replied: "We perform human sacrifices by proxy, you might say—the destruction of human beings who would, let's say, create an antagonistic situation toward us—in the form of curses and hexes."[1] This was not a charge brought against him by some hostile critic; it was an admission he made freely of his own accord.

In Israel, under the Law of Moses, this would have been punishable by death. In our contemporary culture, however, occult practices are not a crime, and there is no penalty attached to them, even if they are used to kill people.

The statement of the Satanist quoted above reveals their use of curses and hexes to kill people, but it by no means absolves them from the charge of performing human sacrifices. Gruesome evidence to the contrary is contained in the following report from the *New York Times*, which ran April 12, 1989, dateline Matamoros, Mexico:

> On Tuesday, . . . officials [Mexican and U.S.] found the bodies of 12 people, including a 21-year-old University of Texas student who had vanished here a month ago, in eight crude graves on [a remote ranch near the U.S. border]. Today, at news conferences here and in Brownsville, Texas, the officials said that a drug gang, seeing human sacrifice as "a magical shield" that would protect it from the police, was responsible for the murders. . . .
>
> Among the suspects still at large is an accused drug smuggler identified as Adolfo de Jesus Constanzo, a native of Cuba, whom the others call El Padrino—the godfather. The police said he ordered the ritual murders, pointing out young men at random on city streets for his followers to abduct, then murder and mutilate on the ranch.
>
> The officials described the murders as a twisted blend of sacrificial and black magic practices from Haiti, Cuba and Jamaica. . . .

There have also been reports from various places in the United States of the sacrifice of infants and small children, carried out by Satanists as part of their rituals.

The primary targets of satanic curses and other occult weapons are the servants of God and Jesus Christ. Satanists rightly recognize who their main enemies are, and direct their attacks against them accordingly. This is illustrated vividly by an incident related to me by a minister friend.

A Christian lady known to my friend was eating with her family in a restaurant in New Orleans—which is reported to be the spiritual center for witchcraft in the U.S.A. While at the table, they were approached by Satanists who had entered the restaurant to "witness" in the same way some Christians might do, going from table to table. They were actively recruiting people for Satanism and showed the lady a printed prospectus for the year 1988, outlining the following six-point, worldwide program, which was to be accompanied by fasting and prayer (!):

1. That the Antichrist would manifest himself soon.
2. That ministers, leaders and missionaries would fall.
3. That ministries and works of God would be destroyed.
4. That Christians would become complacent; want peace over and above all; and seek churches that do not preach a full Gospel with pastors that keep peace no matter what the sin.
5. That Christians cease their fasting and prayer.
6. That the gifts of the Holy Spirit be ignored.

This is but one of many evidences that the Church of Jesus Christ is currently under intense, systematic attack by the forces of Satan. What can the Church do? Christ defeated Satan on the cross. How can we, first of all, defend ourselves; and secondly, make Christ's victory a daily reality in our personal lives and in our churches?

Some illuminating answers are provided by the story of Balaam's attempt to bring a curse on Israel. God intervened on behalf of Israel and turned the proposed curse into a blessing. What did God see in the conduct of Israel at that time that moved Him to take His stand against Satan on their behalf?

Here are some important factors that combined to draw God's favor down upon His people:

1. The people of Israel were moving in fulfillment of God's plan for them.
2. They were supernaturally guided, day and night, by a cloud and a pillar of fire. This corresponds to the guidance of the Holy Spirit for New Testament believers (see Romans 8:14).
3. They were a nation under discipline, with God-appointed leaders and God-given laws.
4. Their relationships were carefully ordered according to a divine pattern. This harmonious pattern of relationships was beautifully depicted by Balaam's own visionary description of them in Numbers 24:5–6:

   "How lovely are your tents, O Jacob! Your dwellings, O Israel! Like valleys that stretch out, like gardens by the riverside, like aloes planted by the LORD, like cedars beside the waters."

   Obviously, this was not a literal picture of Israel, since she was encamped at that time in a desert area.
5. Much of the above was due to the fact that a whole generation of unbelieving and disobedient Israelites had been purged out from among them (see Numbers 26:63–65).

What are the lessons to be learned from this picture of Israel? Its main features could be summed up thus: Israel was a community divinely ordered, disciplined and guided,

160

living in harmony with one another. To state it another way, Israel was not just an assembly of individuals each "doing his own thing."

God has not changed in what He looks for in His people; nor has Satan changed in his tactics against God's people. If the Church at this time does not fulfill the requirements for God's favor and protection, there is only one remedy: *The Church must change*.

Unfortunately, however, the record of Balaam's strategy against Israel does not end with total victory for Israel. Having failed in his attempt to bring a curse upon Israel, Balaam resorted to a second tactic. He advised Balak to use the Moabite women as a snare, to entice the men of Israel, first, into sexual immorality and, second, into idolatry. Where Balaam's first tactic had failed, his second succeeded.

After that, he had no need to pronounce a curse upon the Israelites. By breaking God's first commandment, they had brought God's own curse upon themselves, and 24,000 of them perished (see Numbers 25). In Numbers 31:16, Moses states specifically that this came about through the counsel of Balaam.

In 1 Corinthians 10:8 Paul holds up this incident as a warning to believers in the New Testament. The deceitful tactics of Balaam are also mentioned in three other passages of the New Testament: 2 Peter 2:15–16, Jude 11 and Revelation 2:14. Obviously the strategy of Balaam against Israel contains important warnings also for believers in the New Covenant. The central lesson is simple: Christians who are living in disciplined obedience to God and in harmony with each other can look to God for His protection against Satan. But Christians who are undisciplined, disobedient and out of harmony forfeit their claim on God's protection.

Questions for the Study

1. The two attitude extremes toward Satan by Christians are either _ignore_ him or _fear_ him.
2. What is Satan's primary tactic? _deception_
3. True or false: Curses are one of the main weapons used by servants of Satan against the people of God.
4. What was Balaam's second tactic to bring Israel under a curse? _to entice them into idolatry + sexual sin_
5. God does recognize the power of Satan, but He has equipped His own servants with _superior_ [greater] power.
6. Christians who are living in disciplined _obedience_ to God and in _harmony_ with each other can look to God for His protection against Satan.

Life Application

1. Do you believe there are people who are servants of Satan who can place curses on people? Why or why not?
2. What lessons did you learn from the story of Balaam and Israel? How can you use these lessons in your life?
3. What areas of your life need to change so you can enjoy the protection of God in greater measure?

Memory Verse

Owe no one anything except to love one another, for he who loves another has fulfilled the law.

Romans 13:8

Faith Response

Lord Jesus, I desire to be obedient to Your Word and walk in unity and love with the family of God (see 1 Peter 3:8–12).

Answers

1. Ignoring, fearing.
2. Deception.
3. True.
4. To entice them into sin and idolatry, thus causing them to bring a curse on themselves.
5. Superior or greater.
6. Obedience, harmony.

14

Soulish Talk

It is not difficult for Christians to understand that spiritual forces directed against them from servants of Satan would be dangerous and harmful. Many Christians would be surprised, however, to learn that there are situations in which spiritual forces emanating from their fellow believers could also be harmful. Yet in James 3:14–15 the apostle is writing both to and about Christians when he warns:

> But if you have bitter envy and self-seeking in your hearts, do not boast and lie against the truth.
> This wisdom does not descend from above, but is earthly, sensual, demonic.

To describe a certain kind of "wisdom," James uses adjectives on three descending levels: first, "earthly"; below that, "sensual"; and below that, "demonic." The key to understanding the downward process lies in the second adjective, here translated "sensual." The Greek word is *psuchikos*, formed directly from *psuche*, meaning "soul."

The corresponding English word would be "soulish." Translated in this way, it fits in naturally with the Bible's picture of human personality.

In 1 Thessalonians 5:23 Paul prays: "Now may the God of peace Himself sanctify you completely; and may your whole spirit, soul, and body be preserved blameless." Paul here puts together the three elements that make up a complete human personality, listing them in descending order from the highest to the lowest: first, spirit; then, soul; then, body.

The spirit is that part of human personality that was directly inbreathed by God at creation. It is therefore capable of direct union and communion with the Creator. In 1 Corinthians 6:17 Paul says: "He who is joined to the Lord is *one spirit* with Him" (emphasis added). It would not be correct to say "one soul with Him." Only man's spirit is capable of direct union with God.

In the original pattern of creation, man's spirit related upward to God and downward to his soul. God communicated directly with man's spirit, and through man's spirit with his soul. Together, man's spirit and soul expressed themselves through his body.

At the fall, as a result of man's disobedience, his spirit was cut off from God, and at the same time his soul began to express itself independently of his spirit. This new, "disjointed" relationship was both the consequence and the expression of man's rebellion against God.

Elsewhere in the New Testament, the word *soulish* denotes the activity of man's soul when it is out of its proper relationship to his spirit. It describes, therefore, a condition that is contrary to God's highest will. This can be established by considering briefly two other passages in the New Testament where the word *psuchikos*—that is, "soulish"—occurs.

In 1 Corinthians 2:14–15 Paul says that "the natural [soulish] man does not receive the things of the Spirit of

165

God . . . nor can he know them, because they are spiritually discerned." On the other hand, "he who is spiritual judges all things." It is obvious that "soulish" and "spiritual" are in opposition to each other. The "spiritual" person is functioning according to God's will; the "soulish" person is out of harmony with God. The "soulish" person seeks to apprehend spiritual truth in the realm of his soul, but is unable to do so. The "spiritual" person is united with God through his spirit and is thus able to receive spiritual revelation directly from God.

In Jude 16–19, the apostle describes a class of persons who are associated with the Church, but are nevertheless "grumblers, complainers, walking according to their own lusts" (verse 16). He concludes by saying of them: "These are sensual [soulish] persons, who cause divisions, not having the Spirit [that is, the Holy Spirit]" (verse 19).

Taken together, these passages in 1 Corinthians and in Jude present a consistent picture of a person described as "soulish." He is apparently one who associates with the Church and wears a veneer of spirituality. At the same time, his soul is not rightly related to God through his spirit. In spite of the faith he professes, he is in reality a rebel, out of harmony with God and with the people of God. He is incapable of apprehending spiritual truth. His rebellious attitude and conduct grieve the Spirit of God and cause offense in the Body of Christ.

This analysis explains the descending levels of the corrupt wisdom described in James 3:15: from earthly, to soulish, to demonic. The root problem is rebellion—some form of disobedience to God—some form of rejection of God's authority. This rebellion cuts a person's spirit off from God and from the things of heaven. He is now confined to the plane of earthly values and motives.

At the same time, his soul—out of harmony with God—is exposed by its rebellion to the influence of demons, which his blunted spiritual senses cannot identify. The outcome

166

is a form of wisdom that appears to be "spiritual" but is, in fact, "demonic."

The whole of this third chapter of James focuses on one specific problem: the misuse of the tongue. Furthermore, the entire epistle is addressed mainly—if not exclusively—to those who profess faith in Christ. It is clear, therefore, that this corrupt, counterfeit, demonic wisdom, of which James speaks, finds its expression in words used by Christians. How does such a situation arise?

There are two main areas in which Christians are often guilty in this way on account of the words they utter. The first area is words Christians speak among themselves; the second is words they speak to God—primarily in prayer.

The New Testament gives very clear warnings to Christians as to how they should speak about other people—and especially their fellow believers. In Titus 3:2 Paul says that we are "to speak evil of no one." The phrase *no one* applies to all other people, whether believers or unbelievers.

The Greek verb translated "to speak evil" is *blasphemo*—from which is derived the word *blaspheme*. It is important to understand that the sin of "blasphemy" includes not only evil words spoken against God, but also evil words spoken against our fellow human beings. Whether spoken in reference to God or to other people, such language is forbidden to Christians.

In James 4:11 James deals more specifically with words that Christians speak *about one another*: "Do not speak evil of one another, brethren." The word here translated "to speak evil" is *katalalo*, which means simply "to speak against." Many Christians interpret James to mean that we are not to say anything *false* against other believers. What he actually says, however, is that we are not to speak against fellow believers at all—even if what we say about them is true. The sin that James is dealing with is not speaking *falsely* but speaking *against*.

One of the sins that Christians fall into most easily is *gossip*. In some Christian congregations, if gossip were excluded, scarcely any kind of conversation would be left!

Collins English Dictionary offers the two following definitions of "gossip":

1. Casual and idle chat
2. Conversation involving malicious chatter or rumors about other people

Two of the adjectives here applied to gossip are *idle* and *malicious*. It is not enough for Christians to avoid malice in their talk. In Matthew 12:36 Jesus Himself explicitly warns us against mere idle speech: "But I say to you that for every *idle* word men may speak, they will give account of it in the day of judgment" (emphasis added).

Although the New Testament explicitly forbids gossip, many Christians regard it as a relatively "harmless" sin. Most definitely, however, this is not how God views it. In Romans 1:29–30 Paul lists some of the consequences of man's turning away from God. Here is part of his list: "They are full of envy, murder, strife, deceit and malice. They are gossips, slanderers, God-haters, insolent, arrogant and boastful" (NIV).

The position of *gossips* in this list is significant. Some of the heart attitudes directly associated with gossip are strife, deceit and malice. Gossips themselves are classified with people who are slanderers, God-haters, insolent, arrogant and boastful. Christians who indulge in gossip may think of themselves as "exceptions," but that is not how God sees them.

The danger of this kind of talk is brought out by the descending order of adjectives in James 3:15: earthly, soulish, demonic. Christians who permit themselves to gossip about other people—especially their fellow believers—are directly disobedient to God's Word. As a result, they find themselves on a slippery downward slope. Before they realize what is happening, they have slipped from the "earthly" to the "soulish," and then from the "soulish" to the "demonic."

The words these people speak about others would not normally be described as "curses," but their effect is the same. They are in fact channels through which demonic forces are directed against other members of Christ's Body. Furthermore, it is not only the individuals spoken about who are affected. In James 3:6 the apostle says, "The tongue is so set among our members that it defiles the whole body." The believer who is guilty of this kind of speech actually defiles both himself and that part of the Body of Christ to which he is related.

Some years ago, while in Europe on a ministry trip, I found myself in a situation that gave me vivid new insight into the dangers of soulish talk. I was preparing to speak at a very significant meeting, when I was seized with a crippling pain in my lower abdomen. Fearing that I might have to cancel my commitment to speak that evening, I called out to God for help.

Immediately I had a mental picture of two Christian friends of mine, about six thousand miles away in the United States, talking about me. There was a very warm personal relationship among the three of us, but my two friends had disagreed strongly with a recent course of action I had taken. I sensed that in their conversation they were criticizing me for my action and that their negative words about me were producing the physical symptoms I was struggling against. Furthermore, this was a strategy of Satan to keep me from ministering that evening.

I saw that I needed to do two things. First, by a decision of my will, I forgave my friends for the words they were speaking against me. Then I acted on the promise of Jesus in Matthew 18:18: "Whatever you bind on earth will be bound in heaven, and whatever you loose on earth will be loosed in heaven." With the authority vested in the name of Jesus, I bound the satanic forces at work against me, and then I loosed myself from the effect of my friends' words about me. Within five minutes, the pain in my abdomen had ceased entirely (and never returned!). A few hours later I was able to minister effectively in the meeting, and I had the sense that God's purpose had been fulfilled.

Later, on returning to the United States, I had a meeting with my two friends and the tension between us was resolved. Today the relationship among us is closer than before.

In Matthew 7:1–2 Jesus says: "Judge not, that you be not judged. For with what judgment you judge, you will be judged; and with the measure you use, it will be measured back to you."

It is from the verb translated "to judge" that the English words *critic* and *criticize* are directly derived. When we permit ourselves to criticize other people—especially our fellow believers—in such a way that we are pronouncing judgment on them, we are disobeying Scripture and are thus guilty of a rebellious attitude toward God. This exposes us to the "syndrome" of James 3:15: earthly, soulish, demonic.

If we find ourselves in disagreement with the conduct of a fellow Christian, it is permitted—and sometimes necessary— to follow the pattern of Paul in his disagreement with Peter concerning Judaic practices. In Galatians 2:11 Paul says, "I withstood him [Peter] *to his face*" (emphasis added).

Paul did not criticize Peter's conduct to his own co-workers, Barnabas and Titus. Instead, he went straight to Peter himself and settled his differences with him in person. Had Paul been guilty of criticizing Peter behind his back, the relationship between the two of them might have been permanently fractured. As it was, however, in 2 Peter 3:15—written near the end of Peter's life—he spoke with warm approval of the wisdom given to "our beloved brother Paul."

In Proverbs 27:5 Solomon states this as a principle of conduct: "Better is open rebuke than hidden love" (NIV).

A different kind of situation, in which we may have to speak about another person's wrongdoing, arises when we are legally obligated to serve as a witness. In this case, it is our duty to speak "the truth, the whole truth and nothing but the truth." No one can, however, be at the same time both a witness and a judge. In such a situation, we are not filling the role of a judge, but of a witness. We leave the responsibility of pronouncing judgment to someone else.

The specific sin that Jesus warns us against is taking the position of a judge when God has not assigned that to us. He also warns us that if we do give way to criticizing other people, in due course—from one source or another—the same kinds of criticism we have spoken against others will be leveled against us in our turn.

The Bible's penetrating analysis of the harm caused by misuse of the tongue probably leaves very few among us who would dare to plead "not guilty." If we recognize that we have indeed been guilty of wounding other people with our tongues and thus defiling ourselves and the Body of Christ, we need to repent and to seek God's forgiveness and cleansing. We may also need to ask forgiveness from those we have offended.

Beyond that, we need to learn how to protect ourselves from wounding and hurtful words that others may speak against us. This issue of protection is dealt with in Section 3.

Questions for the Study

1. What are the three elements that make up the human personality? *spirit, soul, body*
2. Which part was directly inbreathed by God at creation? *spirit*
3. Which two characteristics, based on two of the three parts, are in opposition to each other? *soulish* *spiritual*
4. True or false: The sin of blasphemy takes place only when we speak evil against God *or against another*
5. What two adjectives are applied to the word *gossip*? *idle* *malicok*
6. Criticizing fellow believers in such a way as to pronounce judgment on them makes us guilty of a *rebellious* attitude toward God.
7. True or false: The same kind of criticism we speak against others will be leveled against us. *T*

Life Application

1. Describe in your own words "soulish" talk.
2. What are some of the misuses of the tongue?
3. Have you ever participated in soulish talk or misused your tongue? How?
4. Consider asking for forgiveness from those you have offended.

Memory Verse

A man has joy by the answer of his mouth, and a word spoken in due season, how good it is!

Proverbs 15:23

Faith Response

Let the words of my mouth and the meditation of my heart be acceptable in Your sight, O LORD, my strength and my Redeemer (Psalm 19:14).

Answers

1. Spirit, soul, body.
2. Spirit.
3. Soulish and spiritual.
4. False. Blasphemy also refers to evil words spoken against our fellow human beings.
5. Idle, malicious.
6. Rebellious.
7. True.

15

Soulish Prayers

Many Christians are shocked when confronted with the harm they cause by speaking wrongly among themselves about other people. They are still more shocked, however, when confronted with the even greater harm they can cause when they speak wrongly about others *in their prayers to God*. They assume that prayer is always acceptable and its effects are always good. Yet this view is not supported by the Bible.

In Proverbs 28:9, for example, we are warned: "One who turns away his ear from hearing the law, even his prayer is an abomination."

God has laid down in the Bible the principles of prayer that are acceptable to Him. Anyone who ignores these principles and offers prayer that is contrary to them incurs God's displeasure and the rejection of his prayer. In describing God's estimate of this kind of prayer, Solomon uses one of the Bible's strongest terms of disapproval: *abomination*.

Because it is so important for us to pray the right kind of prayers, we dare not depend on our own wisdom. Mercifully, God has not left us to our own devices. He has made available to us a divine Helper: the Holy Spirit. By His enabling we can pray prayers that are acceptable to God. Apart from the Holy Spirit, however, we are incapable of praying in a way that will please God or accomplish His purposes.

In Romans 8:26–27 Paul puts these issues very clearly:

> Likewise the Spirit also helps in our weaknesses. For we do not know what we should pray for as we ought, but the Spirit Himself makes intercession for us with groanings which cannot be uttered. Now He who searches the hearts knows what the mind of the Spirit is, because He makes intercession for the saints according to the will of God.

In our fleshly nature, all of us have certain weaknesses. They are weaknesses not of the body, but of the understanding. They manifest themselves in two related ways. First, we often do not know *what* we should pray for. Second, even when we know *what* to pray for, we do not know *how* to pray for it. We are therefore shut up to total dependence on the Holy Spirit. Only He can show us both the *what* and the *how* of prayer.

In two passages in Ephesians Paul further emphasizes our dependence upon the Holy Spirit to give us prayers that are acceptable to God. In Ephesians 2:18 he stresses that it is only the Holy Spirit who can give us access to God: "For through Him [Jesus] we both [Jews and Gentiles] have *access by one Spirit* [the Holy Spirit] to the Father" (emphasis added). Two conditions for acceptable praying are here combined: *through* Jesus and *by* the Holy Spirit. Each is essential.

There is no natural force that can carry our puny human voices from earth to the very ears of God on His throne in heaven. Only the supernatural power of the Holy Spirit can do that. Without Him, we have no access to God.

Further on, in Ephesians 6:18, Paul again stresses our need for the Holy Spirit's help, particularly in praying for our fellow believers. He says that we should be "praying always with all prayer and supplication *in the Spirit* [the Holy Spirit] . . . for all the saints" (emphasis added). Only prayers prayed *in the Holy Spirit* can call down upon those for whom we pray the help and encouragement they need.

How, then, can we avail ourselves of the Holy Spirit's help? Two primary requirements are *humility* and *purity of motive*. First, we must humble ourselves before the Holy Spirit and acknowledge our need of Him. Then we must allow Him to purge from us all wrong motives and selfish attitudes, and to inspire us with sincere love and concern for those for whom we desire to pray.

The prayers that the Holy Spirit inspires are not necessarily lengthy or eloquent. God is not particularly impressed by fine phrases or a solemn tone of voice. Some of the most effective prayers in the Bible were amazingly simple. When Moses prayed for his sister, Miriam, who had been smitten with leprosy, he simply said, "Please heal her, O God, I pray!" (Numbers 12:13). When the tax collector prayed in the Temple, he uttered only one brief sentence: "God, be merciful to me a sinner!" (Luke 18:13). Yet we know that God heard and answered both these prayers.

If you feel the need to pray, but do not know how to begin, simply ask God for help. Here are some simple words you might use:

> Lord, I need to pray, but I don't know how. Please help me by Your Holy Spirit to pray the kind of prayer You will hear and answer.

After that, accept God's response by faith and pray whatever comes from your heart. Jesus has assured us that if we ask God for bread, He will never give us a stone (see Matthew 7:9).

Suppose, however, we do not submit ourselves to the Holy Spirit and seek His direction. Instead, our prayers are motivated by envy and self-seeking (mentioned in James 3:14) or by other fleshly attitudes, such as resentment, anger, criticism or self-righteousness. The Holy Spirit will not endorse prayers that proceed from such attitudes, nor will He present them before God the Father.

Inevitably, therefore, our praying degenerates into the James 3:15 "syndrome": earthly—soulish—demonic. The effect of such soulish prayers is like that of soulish talk: negative, not positive. It releases against those for whom we are praying invisible, indefinable pressures, which do not relieve their burdens, but rather add to them.

In particular, when we pray for our fellow believers, there are two soulish attitudes we must guard against: We must not *accuse*, and we must not seek to *control*.

It is all too easy to see the faults of other Christians. In fact, this is often what motivates us to pray for them. It is right to pray, but we must be careful how we pray. We are not free to come before God with a catalog of their faults.

When we begin to play the role of accusers, we are following the pattern of Satan, not of Christ. Satan's main title—*devil*—means "slanderer" or "accuser." In Revelation 12:10 he is described as the one who accuses Christians day and night before God. He has been engaged in this task from time immemorial and he is an expert at it. He needs no help from Christians!

I have observed that in almost all the prayers of Paul for his fellow Christians—whether individuals or congregations—he begins by thanking God for them. A remarkable example is provided by the opening to 1 Corinthians. According to what Paul writes later in the letter, there were many kinds of sin in that congregation: strife between the members; carnality; incest; drunkenness at the Lord's Table. Yet Paul opens his letter with eloquent thanksgiving:

177

> I thank my God always concerning you for the grace of
> God which was given to you by Christ Jesus, that you were
> enriched in everything by Him in all utterance and all knowl-
> edge, even as the testimony of Christ was confirmed in you,
> . . . who will also confirm you to the end, that you may be
> blameless in the day of our Lord Jesus Christ.
>
> 1 Corinthians 1:4–6, 8

Giving thanks at the beginning of a prayer has an important psychological effect. It creates a *positive* attitude in
the one who is praying. From such a beginning, it is much
easier to go on praying with positive faith, even though we
are not unaware of serious faults or problems in those for
whom we are praying. For my part, I make it a principle
never to pray for fellow believers without first thanking
God for them. If I cannot do that, then I feel it is better
not to pray at all!

A missionary to India in a previous generation developed
such an effective ministry of prayer that he became known
as "Praying Hyde." On one occasion he was praying for
an Indian evangelist whose ministry lacked both fire and
fruit. He was about to say, "Lord, You know how cold that
brother is." He got as far as the words, "Lord, You know
how . . ." but the Holy Spirit would not allow him to complete his sentence.

Suddenly Hyde realized that it was not his business to
accuse his fellow servant. Instead of focusing on the man's
faults, he began to thank God for everything good he could
find in him. Within months, the Indian brother was dramatically transformed. He became known throughout the
whole area as a dedicated, effective winner of souls.

That is the power of prayer based on positive apprecia-
tion and thankfulness for all that is good in a person. But
suppose Hyde had not been sensitive to the Holy Spirit and
had continued to pray in a negative, condemnatory spirit.
Could not his prayer still have been effective, but in the

opposite direction? Could he not have brought upon his fellow servant such a heavy burden of condemnation that he might never have been able to rise above it?

From time to time, like most other Christians, I experience periods of spiritual "heaviness." In some undefined way, I begin to feel guilty or inadequate or unworthy. Yet I may not be aware of anything specific in my life or conduct to explain these feelings.

In such a situation, I have learned by experience that the cause may not be in me at all. My "heaviness" may be due to some other Christian—well-intentioned but misguided—who is accusing me before God. In particular, the sense of *guilt* is often a warning sign. After all, guilt is the logical outcome of accusation. Once I have correctly diagnosed my problem, I can turn to my High Priest, who sees all my faults and yet continually pleads my case before the Father.

There is hardly such a thing as prayer that is not effective. The question is not whether our prayers are effective. The question is whether their effect is positive or negative. That is determined by the power that works through them. Are they truly from the Holy Spirit? Or are they a soulish counterfeit?

True intercession is based on the pattern of Jesus, as described in Romans 8:33–34:

> Who will bring any charge against those whom God has chosen? It is God who justifies. Who is he that condemns? Christ Jesus, who died—more than that, who was raised to life—is at the right hand of God and is also interceding for us.
>
> NIV

Christ certainly sees our faults as believers more clearly than we see each other's. Yet His intercession on our behalf does not result in our condemnation, but in our justification. He does not establish our guilt, but our righteousness.

Our intercession for our fellow believers should follow the same pattern. Shall we dare to bring a charge against those whom God has chosen? Or to condemn those whom God has justified? Surely that would be presumption in the highest degree!

The message of Scripture is unequivocal. It leaves no room in our prayers for us to accuse our fellow believers. There is, however, a second temptation to misuse the power of prayer, which is more subtle and harder to detect. It takes the form of using prayer to *control* those for whom we pray.

There is something in our fallen, Adamic nature that makes us desire to control other people and to impose our will upon them. In chapter 6 it was pointed out that this desire to control others is the root that produces witchcraft—first as a work of the flesh, and then as an occult practice.

One of the key words that indicates the operation of this force is *manipulation.* There are countless areas in which people may resort to manipulation to get what they want from others. Husbands manipulate their wives, and wives their husbands; children their parents; preachers their congregations; and media advertisers the general public! It is such a common practice that people do not usually recognize it—in themselves or in others.

Nevertheless, manipulation is not the will of God. God Himself never manipulates us, and He never authorizes us to manipulate other people. Whenever we resort to manipulation, we have passed from the realm of the spiritual to that of the soulish. We are operating in a form of wisdom that is not from above.

Because we normally think of prayer as something good and spiritual, we assume that any results we achieve by prayer are necessarily legitimate and must represent the will of God. This is true if the power at work through our prayers is the Holy Spirit. But if our prayers are motivated by our own soulish determination, their effect will be harmful, not beneficial.

Behind this soulish kind of prayer there often lies an arrogant assumption that we have the right to "play God" in the lives of others. In reality, however, any influence that would seek to set aside God's sovereignty over an individual's life is *not* from the Holy Spirit.

There are many different situations in which Christians might be tempted to pray in a way that seems spiritual, but actually is soulish. Here are two typical examples:

1. Accusatory and condemnatory prayers

A church "split" is certain to bring out the soulish element in all parties involved. In this case, Pastor Jones, of the First Full Gospel Church, discovers that his wife is having an affair with Brother Williams, the music minister. He divorces his wife and dismisses Brother Williams.

Brother Williams, however, refuses to admit to the charge of adultery. He complains of "injustice," wins over half the congregation to his side, and starts to build a new church. There follows a lengthy dispute between the two groups concerning the division of the building fund.

A year later Pastor Jones marries again. Brother Williams and his group charge that it is unscriptural for a divorced minister to remarry. They start a special prayer meeting to call down "judgment" upon him.

In the next two years Pastor Jones' new wife twice becomes pregnant, but each time her pregnancy ends in a miscarriage. The gynecologist can find no medical reason for these miscarriages. Brother Williams and his group hail this as the answer to their prayers and God's vindication of their righteous cause.

With their first conclusion I would agree. Their prayers were responsible for the two miscarriages. But what was the

181

power that worked through those prayers? Since the Holy Spirit in Scripture clearly warns us not to judge our fellow believers, He could never lend His authority to prayers with such a motive. The only credible diagnosis that remains is that of James 3:15. The power working through such prayers is earthly, soulish, demonic.

2. Dominating, manipulating prayers

Pastor Strong is accustomed to dominating those around him. He is a widower with two sons and a daughter. He expected both sons to become ministers, but in the end they chose secular careers. Mary, the daughter, remains at home. She is devoted to her father and an active helper in the congregation.

At an evangelistic rally, Mary meets Bob, a Christian worker from another denomination, and they begin a courtship. Pastor Strong is at odds with the church Bob belongs to, however, and opposes the relationship from the beginning. Also, he is fearful of losing Mary's help, at home and in the church. Eventually Mary moves out of her father's home to share an apartment with a girlfriend. Pastor Strong calls this "rebellion." When Mary tells him she is engaged, he sets himself to pray against the planned marriage.

Bob and Mary go ahead with their plans, but the longer they know one another, the more strained their relationship becomes. Neither seems able to relax in the presence of the other. Minor misunderstandings somehow develop into painful clashes. Every activity they plan together ends in inexplicable frustration. Eventually Mary says, "Bob, this can't be God's will for us!" and hands him back his ring.

Mary concludes that the way out of her frustration is to break all contact with professing Christians. Alienated from her father and the church, she follows her brothers

182

into a secular career. Eventually she meets and marries a man who is an agnostic.

How shall we evaluate Pastor Strong's prayers? They were certainly effective, but their effect was harmful. They were the expression of his lifelong desire to dominate those who were close to him. They were powerful enough to break up a relationship that could have brought his daughter happiness and fulfillment. Beyond that, however, they could not bring her back to her faith, or keep her from a subsequent, unscriptual marriage. The power of prayer that brings such negative results does not proceed from the Holy Spirit.

The principles illustrated by these two examples apply to many different kinds of situations in contemporary church life. The lesson they enforce is highly relevant: The power of soulish prayer is both real and dangerous. The result it produces is not a blessing, but a curse.

The sin of soulish praying must be dealt with in the same way as the sin of soulish talking, described in the previous chapter. If we have been guilty, we need to repent and seek God's forgiveness. We may also need to ask forgiveness from people who have been affected by the negative influence of our prayers.

Finally, for the future, we must firmly renounce any attempt either to accuse other people or to control them by the words we speak in prayer.

Questions for the Study ─────────────

1. Only the Holy Spirit can show us _what_ and _how_ to pray for a situation.
2. True or false: Without the Holy Spirit we have no access to God. _T_
3. When we pray for our fellow believers, we must guard against what two soulish attitudes? *accusation* *control*
4. Whenever we resort to manipulation, we have passed from the realm of the _spiritual_ to that of the _soulish_
5. The result of soulish prayers is that they produce _curses_ instead of blessings.

Life Application ─────────────────

1. There are two conditions for acceptable praying: through Jesus and by the Holy Spirit. What does this mean to you? Have you met these conditions?
2. Have you ever used prayer to accuse or control someone as described in this chapter? If so, ask the Lord to forgive you.

Memory Verse ──────────────────

[I] do not cease to give thanks for you, making mention of you in my prayers.

Ephesians 1:16

Faith Response ─────────────────

Father, I rely on the Holy Spirit to guide me in my prayers. Help me when I stray from praying by the Spirit.

Answers

1. What, how.
2. True.
3. Accusation and control.
4. Spiritual, soulish.
5. Curses.

16

Summary of Section 2

The preceding ten chapters have dealt with many of the most important causes of curses as they are revealed in the Bible. It will be helpful to conclude the section with a summary of these causes.

Acknowledging and/or worshiping false gods

All involvement with the occult

Disrespect for parents

All forms of oppression or injustice, especially when directed against the weak and the helpless

All forms of illicit or unnatural sex

Anti-Semitism

Legalism, carnality, apostasy

Theft or perjury

Withholding from God money or other material resources to which He has a claim

Words spoken by people with relational authority, such as father, mother, husband, wife, teacher, priest or pastor

Self-imposed curses

Pledges or oaths that bind people to ungodly associations

Curses that proceed from servants of Satan

Soulish talk directed against other people

Soulish prayers that accuse or seek to control other people

In addition, there are curses for other causes or from other sources, mentioned in Scripture, that are not included in the above list. The most significant of these are listed below in the order in which they occur in the Bible. Various passages that merely reaffirm curses pronounced in Deuteronomy 27 and 28 are not included.

It is noteworthy that the largest category of people who incur God's curse consists of deceptive and unfaithful prophets, priests and teachers. These have been indicated by an asterisk.

A curse on the people of Meroz because they did not join Barak as leader of the Lord's army against Sisera (see Judges 5:23).

A curse from Jotham on those who had murdered the sons of Gideon (see Judges 9:57).

A curse on Jezebel for witchcraft and immorality (see 2 Kings 9:34—compare 2 Kings 9:22).

A curse on those who reject God's commandments through pride (see Psalm 119:21).

A curse on the house of the wicked (see Proverbs 3:33).

A curse on the earth because its inhabitants have defiled it, changing and transgressing God's laws and covenant (see Isaiah 24:5–6).

187

A curse on the people of Edom for persistent enmity and treachery toward Israel (see Isaiah 34:5).

*A curse on false prophets who promised peace to people who were disobeying God (see Jeremiah 29:18).

*A curse on false prophets who commit immorality (see Jeremiah 29:22).

A curse on Israelites who went down to Egypt in defiance of God's warning (see Jeremiah 42:18—compare Jeremiah 44:8, 12).

A curse on any man who fails to carry out the Lord's judgment on His enemies (see Jeremiah 48:10).

*A curse on the blessings of priests who reject God's discipline (see Malachi 2:2).

A curse on "goat" nations who show no mercy to the brothers of Jesus (see Matthew 25:41).

A curse on people who are regularly taught the truth of God, but do not produce appropriate fruit (see Hebrews 6:8).

*A curse on false teachers who are guilty of covetousness, deception and immorality (see 2 Peter 2:14).

Section 3

From Curse to Blessing

Introduction

Have you come to see by now that your life has somehow been blighted by a curse? Are you wondering if there is a way out from under the dark shadow that has been shutting off the sunlight of God's blessing?

Yes, <u>there is a way out!</u> *But there is only one:* through the sacrificial death of Jesus on the cross.

This section will explain in simple, practical terms how you may find and follow God's way—from shadow to sunlight, from curse to blessing.

For your further encouragement you will read—in chapter 20—the story of a man who found the way from frustration and despair to fulfillment and fruitfulness. You can do the same!

This subject matter was a little too heavy for me in the beginning, but then the power of God came on me and I became glued to the message. After a while I felt sweat pouring off my forehead because this teaching was describing exactly what I had experienced. Before the end I began to feel a sense of freedom going through me. The minute I said *Amen!* to the final prayer for the breaking of curses, I felt as if tons of weight had been lifted off me. Praise God!

I am now a full-time minister and God has taken me all over the globe. Everywhere I travel, I have been able to help bring deliverance from curses to countless people who are now walking in the blessings of God.

S. B.

17

The Divine Exchange

The entire message of the Gospel revolves around one unique historical event: the sacrificial death of Jesus on the cross. Concerning this the writer of Hebrews says: "For by one offering [sacrifice] He [Jesus] has perfected forever those who are being sanctified" (Hebrews 10:14). Two powerful expressions are combined: "perfected" and "forever." Together, they depict a sacrifice that comprehends every need of the entire human race. Furthermore, its effects extend throughout time and on into eternity.

It is on the basis of this sacrifice that Paul writes in Philippians 4:19: "And my God shall supply *all your need* according to His riches in glory *by Christ Jesus*" (emphasis added). "All your need" includes, specifically, the release you are seeking from the curse. But first you need to see this as part of a much larger whole—a single, sovereign act of God that brought together all the guilt and the suffering of humanity in one climactic moment of time.

God has not provided many different solutions for the multitudinous problems of mankind. Instead, He offers us one all-sufficient solution, which is His answer to every problem. We may come from many different backgrounds, each of us burdened with our own special need, but to receive God's solution we must all make our way to the same place: the cross of Jesus.

The most complete account of what was accomplished at the cross was given through the prophet Isaiah seven hundred years before it actually took place. In Isaiah 53:10 the prophet depicts a servant of the Lord whose soul was to be offered to God as a sin offering. The writers of the New Testament are unanimous in identifying this unnamed servant as Jesus. The divine purpose accomplished by His sacrifice is summed up in Isaiah 53:6: "All we like sheep have gone astray; we have turned, every one, to his own way; and the LORD has laid on Him the iniquity of us all."

Here is the basic, universal problem of all humanity: We have turned, each of us, to our own way. There are various specific sins that many of us have never committed, such as murder, adultery, theft and so on. But this one thing we all have in common: We have turned to our own way. In so doing, *we have turned our backs on God*. The Hebrew word that sums this up is *avon*, here translated "iniquity." Perhaps the closest equivalent in contemporary English would be "rebellion"—not against man, but against God. In chapter 4 we saw this as the primary cause for the curses listed in Deuteronomy 28.

No one English word, however, whether it is *iniquity* or *rebellion*, conveys the full meaning of *avon*. In its biblical use, *avon* describes not merely iniquity but also the *punishment* or the *evil consequences* that iniquity brings in its train.

In Genesis 4:13, for instance, after God had pronounced judgment on Cain for the murder of his brother, Cain said: "My punishment is greater than I can bear!" The word here translated "punishment" is *avon*. It covered not merely Cain's "iniquity," but also the "punishment" it brought upon him.

In Leviticus 16:22, concerning the scapegoat released on the Day of Atonement, the Lord said: "The goat shall bear on itself all their iniquities to an uninhabited land." In this symbolism, the goat bore not merely the iniquities of the Israelites, but also all the consequences of their iniquities.

In Lamentations 4 *avon* occurs twice with the same meaning. In verse 6 it is translated: "The *punishment of the iniquity* of the daughter of my people" (emphasis added). Again, in verse 22: "The *punishment of your iniquity* . . . O daughter of Zion" (emphasis added). In each case, the single word *avon* is translated by a complete phrase, "the punishment of iniquity." In other words, in its fullest sense *avon* means not simply "iniquity," but also includes *all the evil consequences* God's judgment brings upon iniquity.

This applies to the sacrifice of Jesus on the cross. Jesus Himself was not guilty of any sin. In Isaiah 53:9 the prophet says, "He had done no violence, nor was any deceit in His mouth." But in verse 6 he says, "The LORD has laid on Him the iniquity of us all." Not merely was Jesus identified with our iniquity. He also endured all the evil consequences of that iniquity. Like the scapegoat that had prefigured Him, He carried them away so that they might never return again upon us.

Here is the true meaning and purpose of the cross. On it a divinely ordained exchange took place. First, Jesus endured in our place all the evil consequences that were due by divine justice to our iniquity. Now, in exchange, God offers us all the good that was due to the sinless obedience of Jesus.

Stated more briefly, the evil due to us came upon Jesus so that, in return, the good due to Jesus might be offered to us. God is able to offer this to us without compromising His own eternal justice, because Jesus has already endured on our behalf all the just punishment due to our iniquities.

All of this proceeds solely out of the unfathomable grace of God, and it is received solely by faith. There is no logical explanation in terms of cause and effect. None of us has ever done anything to deserve such an offer, and none of us can ever do anything to earn it.

Scripture reveals many different aspects of the exchange, and many different areas in which it applies. In each case, however, the same principle holds good: *The evil came upon Jesus that the corresponding good might be offered to us*.

The first two aspects of the exchange are revealed in Isaiah 53:4–5:

> Surely He has borne our griefs [literally, sicknesses] and carried our sorrows [literally, pains]; yet we esteemed Him stricken, smitten by God, and afflicted. But He was wounded for our transgressions, He was bruised for our iniquities; the chastisement [punishment] for our peace was upon Him, and by His stripes [wounds] we are healed.

Two truths are here interwoven. The application of one is spiritual and the other physical. On the spiritual plane, Jesus received the punishment due to our transgressions and iniquities that we, in turn, might be forgiven and so have peace with God. (See Romans 5:1.) On the physical plane, Jesus bore our sicknesses and pains that we through His wounds might be healed.

The physical application of the exchange is confirmed in two passages of the New Testament. Matthew 8:16–17 refers to Isaiah 53:4 and records that Jesus "healed all who were sick, that it might be fulfilled which was spoken by Isaiah the prophet, saying: 'He Himself took our infirmities and bore our sicknesses.'"

Again, in 1 Peter 2:24, the apostle refers to Isaiah 53:5–6 and says of Jesus: "[He] Himself bore our sins in His own body on the tree, that we, having died to sins, might live for righteousness—by whose stripes [wounds] you were healed."

The twofold exchange described in the above verses may be summed up as follows:

194

Jesus was punished that we might be forgiven. Jesus was wounded that we might be healed.

A third aspect of the exchange is revealed in Isaiah 53:10, which states that the Lord made the soul of Jesus "an offering for sin." This must be understood in the light of the Mosaic ordinances for various forms of sin offering. The person who had sinned was required to bring his sacrificial offering—a sheep, a goat, a bull or some other animal—to the priest. He would confess his sin over the offering, and the priest would symbolically transfer the sin he had confessed from the person to the animal. Then the animal would be killed, thus paying the penalty for the sin that had been transferred to it.

In the foreknowledge of God, all this was designed to foreshadow what was to be accomplished by the single, all-sufficient sacrifice of Jesus. On the cross, the sin of the whole world was transferred to the soul of Jesus. The outcome is described in Isaiah 53:12: "He poured out His soul unto death." By His sacrificial, substitutionary death, Jesus made atonement for the sin of the whole human race.

In 2 Corinthians 5:21 Paul refers to Isaiah 53:10 and at the same time he also presents the positive aspect of the exchange: "For He [God] made Him [Jesus] who knew no sin to be sin for us, that we might become the righteousness of God in Him."

Paul does not speak here about any kind of righteousness that we can achieve by our own efforts, but about God's own righteousness—a righteousness that has never known sin. None of us can ever earn this. It is as high above our own righteousness as heaven is above earth. It can be received solely by faith.

This third aspect of the exchange may be summed up as follows:

> *Jesus was made sin with our sinfulness that we might become righteous with His righteousness.*

The next aspect of the exchange is a logical outworking of the previous one. The entire Bible, in both the Old Testament and the New, emphasizes that the final outcome of sin is death. In Ezekiel 18:4 the Lord states, "The soul who sins shall die." In James 1:15 the apostle says, "Sin, when it is full-grown, brings forth death." When Jesus became identified with our sin, it was inevitable that He should also experience the death that is the outcome of sin.

In confirmation of this, in Hebrews 2:9, the writer says that "Jesus . . . was made a little lower than the angels, for the suffering of death . . . that He, by the grace of God, might taste death for everyone." The death that He died was the inevitable outcome of human sin that He had taken upon Himself. He bore the sin of all men, and so died the death due to all men.

In return, to all who accept His substitutionary sacrifice, Jesus now offers the gift of eternal life. In Romans 6:23 Paul sets the two alternatives side by side: "For the wages [just reward] of sin is death, but the [unearned] gift of God is eternal life in Christ Jesus our Lord."

Thus the fourth aspect of the exchange may be summed up as follows:

> *Jesus died our death that we might share His life.*

A further aspect of the exchange is stated by Paul in 2 Corinthians 8:9: "For you know the grace of our Lord Jesus Christ, that though He was rich, yet for your sakes He became poor, that you through His poverty might become rich." The exchange is clear: from poverty to riches. Jesus became poor that we in return might become rich.

When did Jesus become poor? Some people picture Him as poor throughout His earthly ministry, but this is not accurate. He Himself did not carry a lot of cash, but at no time did He lack anything He needed. When He sent His disciples out on their own, they likewise lacked nothing (see Luke 22:35). So far from being poor, He and His disciples made a regular practice of giving to the poor (see John 12:4–8; 13:29).

True, Jesus' methods of obtaining money were sometimes unconventional, but money has the same value, whether withdrawn from a bank or the mouth of a fish! (see Matthew 17:27). His methods of providing food were also at times unconventional, but a man who can provide a substantial meal for five thousand men plus women and children certainly would not be considered poor by normal standards! (see Matthew 14:15–21).

Actually, throughout His earthly ministry, Jesus exactly exemplified "abundance," as defined in chapter 5. He always had all that He needed to do the will of God in His own life. Over and above this, He was continually giving out to others, and His supply was never exhausted.

So when did Jesus become poor for our sakes? The answer is: *on the cross.* In Deuteronomy 28:48 Moses summed up absolute poverty in four expressions: hunger, thirst, nakedness and need of all things. Jesus experienced all this in its fullness on the cross.

He was *hungry.* He had not eaten for nearly 24 hours.

He was *thirsty.* One of His last utterances was: "I thirst!" (John 19:28).

He was *naked.* The soldiers had taken all His clothes from Him (see John 19:23).

He was *in need of all things.* He no longer owned anything whatever. After His death He was buried in a borrowed robe and in a borrowed tomb (see Luke 23:50–53). Thus, Jesus, exactly and completely, endured *absolute poverty* for our sakes.

In 2 Corinthians 9:8 Paul presents more fully the positive side of the exchange: "And God is able to make all grace

197

abound toward you, that you, always having all sufficiency in all things, may have an abundance for every good work."[1] Paul is careful to emphasize throughout that the only basis for this exchange is God's *grace*. It can never be earned. It can be received only by faith.

Very often our "abundance" will be like that of Jesus' while He was on earth. We shall not carry large amounts of cash, or have large deposits in a bank. But from day to day we shall have enough for our own needs and something over for the needs of others.

One important reason for this level of provision is indicated by the words of Jesus quoted in Acts 20:35: "It is more blessed to give than to receive." God's purpose is that all His children should be able to enjoy the greater blessing. He provides us, therefore, with enough to cover our own needs and also to give to others.

This fifth aspect of the exchange may be summed up:

Jesus became poor with our poverty that we might become rich with His riches.

The exchange at the cross covers also the emotional forms of suffering that follow from man's iniquity. Here again, Jesus endured the evil that we in turn might enjoy the good. Two of the cruelest wounds brought upon us by our iniquity are *shame* and *rejection*. Both of these came upon Jesus on the cross.

Shame can vary in intensity from acute embarrassment to a cringing sense of unworthiness that cuts a person off from meaningful fellowship either with God or with man. One of the commonest causes—becoming more and more prevalent in our contemporary society—is some form of sexual abuse or molestation in childhood. Often this leaves scars that can be healed only by the grace of God.

Speaking of Jesus on the cross, the writer of Hebrews says that He "endured the cross, *despising the shame*" (Hebrews 12:2, emphasis added). Execution on a cross was the most shameful of all forms of death, reserved for the lowest class of criminal. The person to be executed was stripped of all his clothing and exposed naked to the gaze of passersby, who jeered and mocked. This was the degree of shame Jesus endured as He hung on the cross (see Matthew 27:35–44).

In place of the shame Jesus bore, God's purpose is to bring those who trust in Him to share His eternal glory. In Hebrews 2:10 the writer says: "For it was fitting for Him [God] . . . *in bringing many sons to glory*, to make the captain of their salvation [that is, Jesus] perfect through sufferings" (emphasis added). The shame Jesus endured on the cross has opened the way for all who trust in Him to be released from their own shame. Not only that, but He then shares with us the glory that belongs to Him by eternal right!

There is another wound that is often even more agonizing than shame. It is *rejection*. Usually this stems from some form of broken relationship. In its earliest form, it is caused by parents who reject their own children. The rejection may be active, expressed in harsh, negative ways, or it may be merely a failure to show love and acceptance. If a pregnant woman entertains negative feelings toward the infant in her womb, the child will probably be born with a sense of rejection—which may follow it into adulthood and even to the grave.

The breakup of a marriage is another frequent cause of rejection. This is pictured vividly in the words of the Lord in Isaiah 54:6: "'The LORD will call you back as if you were a wife deserted and distressed in spirit—a wife who married young, only to be rejected,' says your God" (NIV).

God's provision for healing the wound of rejection is recorded in Matthew 27:46, 50, which describes the culmination of the agony of Jesus:

And about the ninth hour Jesus cried out with a loud voice, saying, "Eli, Eli, lama sabachthani?" that is, "My God, My God, why have You forsaken Me?"

. . . Jesus cried out again with a loud voice, and yielded up His spirit.

For the first time in the history of the universe, the Son of God called out to His Father and received no response. So fully was Jesus identified with man's iniquity that the uncompromising holiness of God caused Him to reject even His own Son. In this way Jesus endured rejection in its most agonizing form: rejection by a father. Almost immediately after that, He died, not of the wounds of crucifixion, but of a broken heart. Thus He fulfilled the prophetic picture of the Messiah given in Psalm 69:20: "Reproach has broken my heart."

The record of Matthew continues immediately: "Then, behold, the veil of the temple was torn in two from top to bottom" (Matthew 27:51). This demonstrated symbolically that the way had been opened for sinful man to enter into direct fellowship with a holy God. The rejection of Jesus had opened the way for us to be accepted by God as His children. This is summed up by Paul in Ephesians 1:5–6: "Having predestined us to adoption as sons by Jesus Christ to Himself . . . He [God] made us *accepted in the Beloved*" (emphasis added). The rejection of Jesus resulted in our acceptance.

God's remedy for shame and rejection has never been needed more desperately than it is today. My estimate is that at least one-quarter of the adults in America today suffer from wounds of shame or rejection. It has given me measureless joy to point such people to the healing that flows from the cross of Jesus.

The two emotional aspects of the exchange at the cross that have been analyzed above may be summarized as follows:

200

> *Jesus bore our shame that we might share His glory.*
> *Jesus endured our rejection that we might have His acceptance as children of God.*

The aspects of the exchange analyzed above cover some of humanity's most basic and urgent needs, but they are by no means exhaustive. Actually, there is no need resulting from man's rebellion that is not covered by the same principle of exchange: *The evil came upon Jesus that the good might be offered to us*. Once we have learned to apply this principle in our lives, it releases God's provision for every need.

Now you must lay hold of this principle to meet that special need in your life: *release from the curse*. Paul describes the relevant aspect of the exchange in Galatians 3:13–14:

> Christ has redeemed us from the curse of the law, having become a curse for us (for it is written, "Cursed is everyone who hangs on a tree"), that the blessing of Abraham might come upon the Gentiles in Christ Jesus, that we might receive the promise of the Spirit through faith.

Paul applies to Jesus on the cross an enactment of the Law of Moses, stated in Deuteronomy 21:23, according to which a person executed by hanging on a "tree" (a wooden gibbet) thereby came under the curse of God. Then he points to the resulting opposite: the blessing.

It does not require a theologian to analyze this aspect of the exchange:

> *Jesus became a curse that we might receive a blessing.*

The curse that came upon Jesus is defined as "the curse of the Law." It includes every one of the curses, listed by Moses in Deuteronomy 28, which were examined in chapter 4. Every one of these curses, in its fullness, came upon Jesus. He has thus opened the way for us to obtain

Thank you, Jesus

an equally full release and to enter into the corresponding blessings.

Try for a moment to picture Jesus as He hung there on the cross. Then you will begin to appreciate the full horror of the curse.

Jesus had been rejected by His own countrymen, betrayed by one of His disciples and abandoned by the rest (though some later returned to follow His final agony). He was suspended naked between earth and heaven. His body was wracked by the pain of innumerable wounds, His soul weighed down by the guilt of all humanity. Earth had rejected Him, and heaven would not respond to His cry. As the sun withdrew its light and darkness covered Him, His lifeblood ebbed out onto the dusty, stony soil. Yet out of the darkness, just before He expired, there came one final, triumphant cry: "It is finished!"

In the Greek text that phrase, "It is finished," consists of only one word. It is the perfect tense of a verb that means "to make something complete or perfect." In English, it could be rendered "It is completely complete" or "It is perfectly perfect."

Jesus had taken upon Himself every evil consequence that rebellion had brought upon humanity. He had exhausted every curse of God's broken Law. All this, that we in turn might receive every blessing due to His obedience. Such a sacrifice is stupendous in its scope, yet marvelous in its simplicity.

Have you been able to accept with faith this account of the sacrifice of Jesus and of all that He has obtained for you? In particular, if you are living under the shadow of a curse, have you begun to see that Jesus, at infinite cost to Himself, has made full provision for your release?

If so, there is one immediate response that you need to make—a response that is the simplest and purest expression of true faith. It is to say, "Thank You!"

202

Do that right now! Say, "Thank You! Thank You, Lord Jesus, for all that You have done for me! I do not fully understand, but I do believe, and I am grateful."

Now keep on thanking Him in your own words. The more you thank Him, the more you will believe what He has done for you. And the more you believe, the more you will want to thank Him.

Giving thanks is the first step to release.

Questions for the Study

1. What is the one unique historical event around *the crucifix-* which the entire message of the Bible revolves?
2. True or false: God supplies many different solutions for the problems of mankind. *F only one*
3. In Deuteronomy 28:48 Moses sums up four expressions of absolute poverty. What are they? *hunger, thirst, nakedness, poverty, need of all things*
4. Two of the cruelest wounds brought on us by our iniquity are **shame** and **rejection**
5. List the eight exchanges at the cross mentioned in this chapter.
6. As a result of the exchange at the cross, Jesus became a **curse** so that we might receive a **blessing**
7. What is the first step to release? *giving thanks*

Life Application

1. Do you believe Jesus went to the cross for your sins?
2. How have you personally experienced His sacrifice in your life?
3. Of the eight exchanges mentioned, are there any you have not experienced? If yes, which ones, and why do you think that is?

Memory Verse

My God shall supply all your need according to His riches in glory by Christ Jesus.

Philippians 4:19

Faith Response

Jesus, I accept all You did for me on the cross. I believe that every one of my needs is met in You.

Answers

1. The sacrificial death of Jesus Christ on the cross.
2. False. He offers us only one that is all-sufficient: the cross of Jesus.
3. Hunger, thirst, nakedness and need of all things.
4. Shame, rejection.
5. (1) Jesus was punished that we might be forgiven. (2) Jesus was wounded that we might be healed. (3) Jesus was made sin with our sinfulness that we might become righteous with His righteousness. (4) Jesus died our death that we might share His life. (5) Jesus became poor with our poverty that we might become rich with His riches. (6) Jesus bore our shame that we might share His glory. (7) Jesus endured our rejection that we might have His acceptance as children of God. (8) Jesus became a curse that we might receive a blessing.
6. Curse, blessing.
7. Giving thanks.

18

Seven Steps to Release

There is one—and only one—all-sufficient basis for every provision of God's mercy: the exchange that took place on the cross. In the previous chapter, eight main aspects were summarized:

Jesus was punished that we might be forgiven.

Jesus was wounded that we might be healed.

Jesus was made sin with our sinfulness that we might become righteous with His righteousness.

Jesus died our death that we might share His life.

Jesus became poor with our poverty that we might become rich with His riches.

Jesus bore our shame that we might share His glory.

Jesus endured our rejection that we might have His acceptance as children of God.

Jesus became a curse that we might receive a blessing.

This list is not complete. There are other aspects of the exchange that could be added. But all of them are different

206

facets of the provision God has made through the sacrifice of Jesus. The Bible sums them up in one grand, all-inclusive word: *salvation*. Christians often limit salvation to the experience of having one's sins forgiven and being born again. Wonderful though this is, however, it is only the first part of the total salvation revealed in the New Testament.

The full scope of salvation is obscured—at least, in part—by problems of translation. In the original Greek text of the New Testament, the verb *sozo*, normally translated "to save," is also used in a variety of ways that go beyond the forgiveness of sins. It is used, for instance, in many cases of people being physically healed.[1] It is also used of a person being delivered from demons,[2] and of a dead person being brought back to life.[3] In the case of Lazarus, it is used of recovering from a fatal illness.[4] In 2 Timothy 4:18 Paul uses the same verb to describe God's ongoing preservation and protection from evil, which will extend throughout his life.

The total outworking of salvation includes every part of man's being. It is beautifully summed up in Paul's prayer in 1 Thessalonians 5:23: "Now may the God of peace Himself sanctify you completely; and may your whole spirit, soul, and body be preserved blameless at the coming of our Lord Jesus Christ." Salvation includes the total human personality—spirit, soul and body—and it is consummated only by the resurrection of the body at the return of Christ.

No one enters into all the varied provisions of salvation simultaneously, however, or by one single transaction. It is normal to progress by stages from one provision to the next. Many Christians never go beyond receiving forgiveness of their sins. They are not aware of the many other provisions that are freely available to them.

The order in which a person receives the various provisions is determined by the sovereignty of God, who deals with all of us as individuals. The starting point, generally, is forgiveness of sins, but not always. In the earthly ministry of Jesus, people often received physical healing first, and then forgiveness of their sins.

This can still happen today. In 1968 my own wife, Ruth, while still single and living as a practicing Jewess, had lain sick in bed for many weeks. Then she received a miraculous visitation from Jesus in her bedroom and was instantly and totally healed. But it was two years later before she recognized her need to have her sins forgiven. Only then was she born again.

When we come to God on the basis of Christ's sacrifice for us, we need to be sensitive to the leading of the Holy Spirit. We cannot impose our priorities upon God, but we must let Him work with us in the order He chooses. A person may, for instance, be determined to seek financial prosperity, whereas God's first priority for him is righteousness. If he stubbornly insists on claiming prosperity before righteousness, he may not receive either!

Again, a person may seek physical healing, not knowing that the root of his physical sickness is an inner emotional problem—such as rejection or grief or insecurity. In response, God will move to bring the emotional healing that is needed. If the person does not open himself up to this, however, but continues to beg merely for physical healing, he may in the end receive no healing at all, either physical or emotional.

Sometimes God seeks to reveal to us a provision of salvation that is our most urgent need, and yet we are not aware of it. This applies particularly to the provision for release from a curse. Very often a curse over a person's life is the unsuspected barrier that holds him back from the other provisions of salvation. Normally, this barrier must be dealt with first, before other needs can be met.

This is the provision we will now focus upon: *the exchange from curse to blessing*. At this point we are confronted by precisely the same issues Moses put before the Israelites as they were preparing to enter the land of Canaan: "This

208

day I call heaven and earth as witnesses against you that
I have set before you life and death, blessings and curses.
Now choose life, so that you and your children may live"
(Deuteronomy 30:19, NIV). The issues were so solemn, and
so far-reaching in their consequences, that Moses called
heaven and earth to witness Israel's response.

The alternatives were clear: life and blessings, on the
one hand; death and curses, on the other. God required the
Israelites to make their own choice. He urged them to make
the right choice: life and blessings. But He would not make
the choice for them. He also reminded them that the choice
they made would affect not merely their own lives, but also
the lives of their descendants. This emerges once again as
a characteristic feature of both blessings and curses: They
continue from generation to generation.

The choice that Israel made at that time determined their
destiny. The same is true for us today. God sets before us
precisely the same alternative: life and blessings or death
and curses. He leaves it to us to choose. Like Israel, we
determine our destiny by the choice we make. Our choice
may also affect the destiny of our descendants.

I remember when I was first confronted by those words
of Moses. As I realized that God required a response from
me, I was overawed. God was waiting for me to choose! I
could not evade the issue. Not to choose was, in effect, to
make the wrong choice.

I thank God that He gave me the grace to make the right
choice. Never, in all the years since then, have I regretted
it. God soon began to show me, however, the implications
of my choice. I had passed through a door leading to a
lifetime walk of faith and obedience, from which there
was no turning back.

All who desire to pass from curse to blessing must go
through the same door. First, there must be a clear recognition of the issues God sets before us. Then there must
be a simple, positive response: "Lord, on the basis of Your

Word, I make my response. I refuse death and curses, and I choose life and blessings."

Once we have made this choice, we can go on to claim release from any curses over our lives. What are the steps that we must take for this? There is no one set pattern that everyone must follow. In bringing people to the point of release, however, I have found it helpful to lead them through the seven stages outlined below.

You may be approaching this issue from the perspective of one who is concerned to help or counsel others. To receive the full benefit of this instruction, however, I recommend that you put yourself mentally in the place of the person who needs release. In so doing, you may discover that is where *you* actually are!

1. Confess your faith in Christ and in His sacrifice on your behalf.

In Romans 10:9–10 Paul explains that there are two essential conditions for receiving the benefits of Christ's sacrifice: to *believe* in the heart that God raised Jesus from the dead and *confess* with the mouth that He is Lord. Faith in the heart is not fully effective until it has been completed by confession with the mouth.

Literally, the word *confess* means "to say the same as." In the context of biblical faith, confession means saying with our mouth what God has already said in His Word. In Hebrews 3:1 Jesus is called the "High Priest of our confession." When we make the right scriptural confession concerning Him, it releases His priestly ministry on our behalf.

To receive the benefits of Christ's sacrifice, we need to make our confession specific and personal. For example:

> Lord Jesus Christ, I believe that You are the Son of God and the only way to God; and that You died on the cross for my sins and rose again from the dead.

2. Repent of all your rebellion and your sins.

There may have been many external factors—even going back to previous generations—that have contributed to the curse over your life. Nevertheless, the root of all your problems lies within yourself. It is summed up in that one word *avon* (iniquity): your rebellious attitude toward God and the sins that have resulted from it. For this, you must accept personal responsibility.

Before you can receive God's mercy, therefore, He requires that you *repent*. This must be a deliberate decision on your part: You lay down your rebellion and submit yourself without reservation to all that God requires of you. A person who has truly repented no longer argues with God!

The New Testament leaves no room for faith that bypasses repentance. When John the Baptist came to prepare the way before Jesus, the first word in his message was *"Repent . . .!"* (Matthew 3:2, emphasis added). Later, when Jesus commenced His public ministry, He took up where John had left off: *"Repent, and believe in the gospel"* (Mark 1:15, emphasis added). *Without repentance, no effective faith is possible.* Many professing Christians are continually struggling for faith because they have never fulfilled the prior condition of repentance. Consequently, they never receive the full benefits of Christ's sacrifice.

Here is a suggested confession that expresses the repentance that God demands:

> I give up all my rebellion and all my sin, and I submit myself to You as my Lord.

3. Claim forgiveness of all sins.

The great barrier that keeps God's blessing out of our lives is *unforgiven sin*. God has already made provision for our sins to be forgiven, but He will not do this until we

211

confess them. *"If we confess our sins*, He is faithful and just to forgive us our sins and to cleanse us from all unrighteousness" (1 John 1:9, emphasis added). God is *faithful* to do this because He has given us His promise, and He always keeps His promises. He is also *just* because the full penalty for our sins has already been paid by Jesus.

It may be that God has shown you certain sins that opened you up to a curse. If so, make a specific confession of those sins.

It is also possible that a curse has come upon you because of sins committed by your ancestors (especially idolatry or the occult). You do not bear the guilt of sins your ancestors committed, but you may be affected in various ways by the consequences of their sins. If you know this to be the case, ask God also for release from those consequences.

Here is a suitable prayer that covers this:

> I confess all my sins before You and ask for Your forgiveness—especially for any sins that exposed me to a curse. Release me also from the consequences of my ancestors' sins.

4. Forgive all other people who have ever harmed you or wronged you.

Another great barrier that can keep God's blessing out of our lives is *unforgiveness* in our hearts toward other people. In Mark 11:25 Jesus put His finger on this as something that we must deal with, if we expect God to answer our prayers: "And whenever you stand praying, if you have anything against anyone, forgive him, that your Father in heaven may also forgive you your trespasses."

The same principle runs all through the New Testament: If we want God to forgive us, we must be prepared to forgive others.

Forgiving another person is not primarily an emotion; it is a *decision*. I sometimes illustrate this with a little "parable." You have in your hand IOUs from another person that total $10,000. In heaven, however, God has in His hand IOUs from you to Him in the amount of $10,000,000. God makes you an offer: "You tear up the IOUs in your hand, and I'll tear up the IOUs in Mine. On the other hand, if you hold onto your IOUs, I'll hold onto Mine!"

Understood in this way, forgiving another person is not a tremendous sacrifice. It is merely enlightened self-interest. Anyone who is not willing to cancel a debt of $10,000 in order to have his own debt of $10,000,000 canceled is lacking in business sense!

God may now be bringing to your mind some person or persons whom you need to forgive. If so, you can look to the Holy Spirit for help. He will prompt you to make the right decisions, but He will not make them for you. While you feel His prompting, respond. Make a clear-cut decision to forgive. Then verbalize your decision. Say out loud, "Lord, I forgive . . ." and name the person or persons involved. The ones you find it hardest to name are the ones you most need to forgive! Here are some simple words you can use:

> By a decision of my will, I forgive all who have harmed me or wronged me—just as I want God to forgive me. In particular, I forgive . . . [name the person or persons].

5. Renounce all contact with anything occult or satanic.

Before you come to the actual prayer of release, there is one further, important area that must be dealt with: all contact with anything occult or satanic. This includes a very wide range of activities and practices. You may need to turn back for a moment to pages 77–79 in chapter 6, where there is a list that covers some, but not all, of the forms that these may take. If you are unclear about an area that is not mentioned in the list, ask God to make it clear to you.

If you have been involved at any time in such activities or practices, you have crossed an invisible border into the kingdom of Satan. Since that time, whether you know it or not, Satan has regarded you as one of his subjects. He considers that he has a legal claim to you. Since the Kingdom of God and the kingdom of Satan are in total opposition to one another, you cannot enjoy the full rights and benefits of a citizen in God's Kingdom until you have finally and forever severed all connection with Satan and totally canceled any claim he may have against you.

In 2 Corinthians 6:14–15 Paul stresses the necessity of a complete break with Satan's kingdom: "What fellowship can light have with darkness? What harmony is there between Christ and Belial [that is, Satan]?" (NIV). In verse 17 he concludes with a direct charge from the Lord Himself: "Therefore 'Come out from among them and be separate, says the Lord. Do not touch what is unclean, and I will receive you.'"

Making this break requires also that you deal with any "contact objects"—that is, objects that would still link you with Satan. This could include many different items. In my case, as I related in chapter 2, it was the Chinese dragons I had inherited. If you have any doubts about how this might apply in your situation, ask God to put His finger on anything that is offensive to Him. Then get rid of it in the most effective way: Burn it, smash it, throw it into deep water—or whatever!

If you are ready to make this total break with Satan and his kingdom, here is an appropriate way to affirm it:

I renounce all contact with anything occult or satanic—if I have any "contact objects," I commit myself to destroy them. I cancel all Satan's claims against me.

6. You are now ready to pray the prayer of release from any curse.

If you have been willing to commit yourself to each of the preceding five steps, you are now at the place where you can pray the actual prayer of release from any curse over your life. But remember, there is only one basis upon which God offers His mercy: the exchange that took place when Jesus died on the cross. Included in that exchange was provision for release from every curse. By being hanged on a cross, Jesus became a curse with every curse that could ever come upon you, that you in turn might be released from every curse and receive God's blessing in its place.

It is important that you base your faith *solely* upon what Jesus obtained for you through His sacrifice on the cross. You do not have to "earn" your release. You do not have to be "worthy." If you come to God with thoughts like that, you will have no solid basis for your faith. God responds to us only on the basis of what Jesus has done on our behalf, not of any merits we may fancy we have in ourselves.

If you pray with this basis for your faith, your prayer should end not merely with asking, but with actually receiving. In Mark 11:24 Jesus established this as a principle: "Therefore I tell you, whatever you ask for in prayer, *believe that you have received it,* and it will be yours" (NIV, emphasis added).

In this kind of prayer there are two distinct stages, related as cause and effect: *receiving* and *having. Receiving* is the cause, from which *having* follows as the effect. *Receiving* is in the past tense; *having* is in the future. *Receiving* takes place when we pray. Then *having* follows at a time and in a way determined by God's sovereignty. But the principle Jesus emphasizes is this: If we do not *receive* at the time we pray, we have no assurance that we will ever *have*.

Here is a prayer that would be appropriate. You might first read through this prayer and then read on for further instructions.

215

Prayer of Release

> Lord Jesus, I believe that on the cross You took on Yourself every curse that could ever come upon me. So I ask You now to release me from every curse over my life—in Your name, Lord Jesus Christ!
>
> By faith I now receive my release and I thank You for it.

Now, pause for a moment! Before you pray this prayer of release, you would be wise to reaffirm each of the five preceding confessions you have already made. To make this easier for you, they are repeated below, but without any added comments or explanation.

Read them out loud, slowly and deliberately, with undivided attention. If you feel uncertainty about any section, go back and read it again. Identify yourself with the words you utter. By the time you have read them through, *you should have the sense that you have brought yourself to God* with the words you have spoken. Then go straight on into the prayer of release, which is repeated at the end.

Here, then, is the complete prayer:

Lord Jesus Christ, I believe that You are the Son of God and the only way to God; and that You died on the cross for my sins and rose again from the dead.

I give up all my rebellion and all my sin, and I submit myself to You as my Lord.

I confess all my sins before You and ask for Your forgiveness—especially for any sins that exposed me to a curse. Release me also from the consequences of my ancestors' sins.

By a decision of my will, I forgive all who have harmed me or wronged me—just as I want God to forgive me. In particular, I forgive. . . .

I renounce all contact with anything occult or satanic—if I have any "contact objects," I commit myself to destroy them. I cancel all Satan's claims against me.

Lord Jesus, I believe that on the cross You took on Yourself every curse that could ever come upon me. So I ask You now to release me from every curse over my life—in Your name, Lord Jesus Christ!

By faith I now receive my release and I thank You for it.

Now don't stop at saying "Thank You" just once or twice. Your *mind* cannot grasp a fraction of what you have asked God to do for you, but respond to God with your *heart*! This could be the time to release hurts or pressures or inhibitions that have built up inside you over the years. If a dam breaks inside you, don't try to hold back the tears that are the outflow of your heart.

Don't be held back by self-consciousness or embarrassment! God has known all along the things that you kept shut up inside you—and He is not the least embarrassed by them. So why should you be? Tell God how much you really love Him. The more you express your love, the more real it will become to you.

On the other hand, there is no set pattern for responding to God that everyone has to follow. The key to release is not some particular type of response. Faith can be expressed in many different ways. Just be your real self with God. Open your whole being to God's love as a flower opens its petals to the sun.

7. Now believe that you have received, and go on in God's blessing!

Do not try at this stage to analyze what form the blessing will take or how God will impart it to you. Leave that in God's hands. Let Him do it just how and when He will. You do not have to concern yourself with that. Your part is simply to open yourself, without reservation, to all that God wants to do in you and for you through His blessing.

217

Remember that God "is able to do exceedingly abundantly above all that we ask or think" (Ephesians 3:20). So do not limit God to doing only what you think.

Here is a simple form of words that you can use:

> Lord, I now open myself to receive Your blessing in every way You want to impart it to me.

It will be exciting for you to see just how God will respond!

Questions for the Study

1. Salvation includes which parts of the human personality? *spirit, soul, body*
2. In Jesus' earthly ministry people often received *physical healing* first, and then forgiveness of their *sins*.
3. Often a curse over a person's life is the *unsuspected barrier* that holds him back from the other provisions of salvation.
4. True or false: Faith in the heart is not fully effective until it has been completed by confession with the mouth. *T*
5. Without *repentance* no effective faith is possible. *① unforgiven sin*
6. What are three great barriers that keep God's blessing out of our lives? *② unforgiveness ③ contact c occult*
7. Forgiving another person is not primarily an emotion; it is a *decision*
8. True or false: All contact with anything occult or satanic must be dealt with before you can pray the actual prayer of release. *T*
9. List the seven steps to release.

Life Application

1. Are you ready to follow the seven steps to be released from curses over your life? If not, why not?
2. Follow the seven steps. Don't rush them; take your time at each step. Review your answers in the Life Application sections in this self-study course (at the end of each chapter), and use the prayer on pages 216–17 as an example of how to pray. (1) Confess your faith in Christ. (2) Repent. (3) Claim forgiveness according to 1 John 1:9. (4) Forgive others (including anyone you mentioned in the Life Application sections from chap-

ters 7 and 11 who has wronged you). (5) Renounce contact by you or members of your family from generations past with the occult, false religions, secret societies or idols. (6) Pray the prayer of release. (7) Receive in faith.

Memory Verse

If the Son makes you free, you shall be free indeed.

John 8:36

Faith Response

Jesus, I will stand fast in the freedom with which You have made me free. I will not again be held in bondage. (See Galatians 5:1.)

Answers

1. Spirit, soul, body.
2. Physical healing, sins.
3. Unsuspected barrier.
4. True.
5. Repentance.
6. Unforgiven sin (step 3), unforgiveness (step 4) and occult contact (step 5).
7. Decision.
8. True.
9. (1) Confess your faith in Christ and in His sacrifice on your behalf. (2) Repent of all your rebellion and sins. (3) Claim forgiveness. (4) Forgive everyone who has harmed or wronged you. (5) Renounce all contact with anything occult or satanic. (6) Pray the prayer of release from any curse. (7) Believe that you have received and go on in God's blessing.

19

From Shadows to Sunlight

If you followed the instructions in the previous chapter, you have crossed an invisible boundary. Behind you now is a territory overshadowed by curses of many different kinds and from many different sources. Before you lies a territory made bright by the sunshine of God's blessings. Before you go any further, cast your mind back to the summary of the list Moses gave in Deuteronomy 28:2–13:

- Exaltation
- Health
- Reproductiveness
- Prosperity
- Victory
- God's favor

These are all parts of your inheritance in Christ, waiting for you to explore and to claim.

It could help you to repeat these key words over to your-self several times—preferably out loud. Living under a curse often makes it difficult for a person to envisage what it would be like to enjoy the corresponding blessing. Ask God to make your new inheritance real and vivid to you. You may need to go on repeating these words frequently—even many times a day—until you really know they are yours!

As you repeat them, pause and thank God that each one is now part of your inheritance. Remember that giving thanks is the purest and simplest expression of faith. If you have had a long struggle with a curse over your life, there may be areas of your mind from which the darkness is not immediately dispelled. Repeating these positive words that describe the blessings will be like seeing the first rays of the sun shining into a dark valley, then spreading until the whole valley is illuminated.

The transition from the dark to the sunlit territory may take many different forms. There is no single pattern that is standard for everyone. Some people experience an almost instantaneous release and seem to enter immediately into the blessings that Scripture promises. For others, who are equally sincere, there may be a long, hard struggle. The more deeply people have been involved in the occult, the harder may be their struggle to escape. Satan regards them as his legitimate prey, and he is determined to hold onto them. On their part, they must be even more determined to assert their claim to the freedom that has been purchased for them by the sacrifice of Jesus.

Also, Satan has at least some foreknowledge of what God has prepared for those who escape from his oppression. The greater the blessings in store for a person, the more deter-mined will be Satan's attempt to hold him back. Viewed in this light, as foreshadowings of blessings ahead, our strug-gles can actually become a source of encouragement.

Over and above these factors, we are confronted with the sovereignty of God. God's perspective is different from ours. He takes into account factors in a situation about which we know nothing. He always keeps His promises, but in most cases there are two things He does not reveal in advance: the precise way that He will work in each life, and the precise time that He will take. No one can dictate to God exactly how to fulfill His promises. What we must do is maintain an attitude of firm, unwavering trust that God will move when and how He sees fit.

We need to look once more at the positive side of the exchange described by Paul in Galatians 3:13–14:

> Christ has redeemed us from the curse of the law, having become a curse for us (for it is written, "Cursed is everyone who hangs on a tree"), that the blessing of Abraham might come upon the Gentiles in Christ Jesus, that we might receive the promise of the Spirit through faith.

Paul points out three important facts concerning the promised blessing:

First, it is not something vague or undefined. It is quite specific: *the blessing of Abraham*. In Genesis 24:1 its extent is defined: "The LORD had blessed Abraham in *all things*" (emphasis added). God's blessing covered every area of Abraham's life. He has a corresponding blessing prepared for each person who fulfills His conditions.

Second, the blessing comes only *in Christ Jesus*. It cannot be earned by our own merits. It is offered solely upon the basis of our relationship to God through Jesus Christ. There is no other channel through which the blessing can flow into our lives. If the relationship with Christ is ruptured by unbelief or disobedience, the blessing will cease to flow. But thank God, it can be restored immediately by sincere repentance!

Third, the blessing is further defined as *"the promise of the [Holy] Spirit."* Concerning this, Jesus tells us in John 16:13–15:

"But when he, the Spirit of truth, comes, he will guide you into all truth. . . . He will bring glory to me by taking from what is mine and making it known to you. All that belongs to the Father is mine. That is why I said the Spirit will take from what is mine and make it known to you."

NIV

What wonderful words of encouragement! All three Persons of the Godhead—Father, Son and Holy Spirit—are united in their purpose to share with us all that has been purchased for us by the sacrifice of Jesus. Because this is far greater than the natural mind can comprehend, we must depend upon the Holy Spirit to guide us into our full inheritance and to show us how to appropriate what God has provided for us.

In Romans 8:14 Paul again emphasizes the unique role of the Holy Spirit: "For as many as are led by the Spirit of God, these are sons of God." Paul is careful to use here the continuing present tense: "as many as *are continually led* by the Spirit of God." To be "led by the Holy Spirit" is not a single, once-for-all experience. It is something on which we must depend moment by moment. It is the only pathway to spiritual maturity. Through it we grow up from being little children to become *mature sons* of God.

Unfortunately, many Christians never fully enjoy the guidance and companionship of the Holy Spirit for one basic reason: They do not realize that He is a *Person*. "The Lord is the Spirit" (2 Corinthians 3:17). Just as God the Father is Lord, and God the Son is Lord, so also God the Spirit is Lord. He is not just a theological abstraction, nor a set of rules, nor half a sentence at the end of the Apostles' Creed. He is a Person, and He wants us to cultivate an intimate, *personal* relationship with Him.

The Holy Spirit has His own distinctive characteristics. He is not aggressive or "pushy," nor does He shout at us. He usually speaks in soft tones and directs us by gentle

224

impulses. To receive His direction, we must be attentive to His voice and sensitive to His impulses.

Furthermore, the Holy Spirit deals with each of us as individuals. To enter into God's blessings, there is no single set of rules that everybody must follow. Each of us has a special, distinctive personality with unique needs and aspirations, unique strengths and weaknesses. The Holy Spirit respects our uniqueness. Someone has said that God never makes one believer a carbon copy of another. Nor does He produce Christians on a factory assembly line.

Only the Holy Spirit knows the special dangers that threaten us in any situation or the particular blessings that will meet our individual needs. He guides us faithfully through the dangers and opens up to us the blessings. If we begin to follow some religious system or to model ourselves on some other Christian, we shall miss some of the choicest blessings God has marked out for us.

You would be wise, therefore, to pause for a moment and offer up a brief prayer:

Holy Spirit, I open my heart and mind to You. Reveal to me the blessings that Jesus has obtained for me and how I may receive them.

In Hebrews 10:14—already quoted in chapter 17—the writer uses two contrasted tenses to depict two opposite sides of the exchange that took place on the cross. To describe what Jesus accomplished, he uses the *perfect* tense: "By one offering He *has perfected* forever" (emphasis added). What Jesus has done is absolutely and eternally complete. Nothing need ever be added, and nothing can ever be taken away.

On the other hand, to describe the outworking of the sacrifice in those who accept it for themselves, the writer uses the *continuing present*: "those who *are being sanctified*" (emphasis added). Our appropriation of the sacrifice is not immediately complete; it is *progressive*. The process by which we appropriate it is described as "being sanctified"—that is, being set apart to God in holiness. As we bring our lives progressively into line with God's requirements of holiness, we are able to enter into His blessings more fully.

When confronted with this challenge, Christians sometimes respond, "But I thought I got everything when I was born again!" The answer to that is yes—and no. There are two sides to this issue: the legal and the experiential. The answer will differ according to which side we view it from.

Legally, you did indeed "get everything" when you were born again. According to Romans 8:17, when you became a child of God, you were made an heir of God and a joint heir with Christ. Legally, from that point on, you were entitled to share Christ's whole inheritance with Him.

Experientially, however, you were only at the beginning of a process that takes a lifetime to complete. The Christian life could be described as a progression from the legal to the experiential. Step by step, in faith, we must appropriate in experience all that is already ours by legal right through our faith in Christ. This is what the writer of Hebrews calls "being sanctified."

In John 1:12 the apostle says, concerning those who have been born again through receiving Jesus, that God has given them *the right to become children of God* (emphasis added). The Greek word translated "right" is *exousia*, usually translated "authority." That is what a person actually receives at the new birth: *authority to become a child of God*.

Authority is effective, however, only insofar as it is exercised. The potential of the new birth is unlimited, but the actual results depend on the exercise of the authority that goes with it. What a person will become through the new birth is determined by the extent to which he exercises his God-given authority.

There is a close parallel between the experience of believers entering into the blessings of God in the New Covenant and that of the Israelites entering into Canaan under the Old Covenant. In the first covenant, under a leader named Joshua, God brought His people into *a promised land*. In the second covenant, under a leader named Jesus (which is another form of Joshua), God brings His people into *a land of promises*. Just as the land of Canaan was the physical inheritance appointed for Israel, so the promises of God, offered through Jesus, are the spiritual inheritance appointed for Christians in this dispensation. The same principles that applied to Israelites then apply to Christians now.

In Joshua 1:2–3 God gave Joshua instructions on how the Israelites were to take possession of their inheritance:

> "Moses My servant is dead. Now therefore, arise, go over this Jordan, you and all this people, to the land which I am giving to them—the children of Israel. Every place that the sole of your foot will tread upon I have given you, as I said to Moses."

There is precisely the same contrast of tenses here as in Hebrews 10:14. In verse 2 of Joshua 1, the Lord uses the continuing present: "I *am giving* [the land]" (emphasis added). But in verse 3 He uses the perfect tense: "I *have given* [the land]" (emphasis added). From verse 3 onward, the legal ownership of Canaan was settled: It belonged to Israel. Experientially, however, nothing had changed. The Canaanites were still in occupation of the land.

The challenge to Joshua and his people was to move from the legal to the experiential. This they were to do one step at a time. As they placed their feet on each place, it became theirs not just legally, but in actual experience.

Had the Israelites responded to God's promise in the same way that some Christians would like to, history would

227

have been very different. They would have lined up on the east bank of the Jordan, folded their arms, looked westward and said, "It's all ours!" But the Canaanites would have laughed at them. They knew who still had possession of the land.

As it was, Joshua and his people acted very differently. First they crossed the Jordan by a miracle that God performed in response to their obedience. Then they besieged and captured Jericho—again by a miracle. But after that their further progress was mainly by battles, not by miracles. They moved out in every direction across Canaan and fought a long series of battles against the various inhabitants of the land. Even after much arduous warfare, their task had not been completed. A long time later, God said to Joshua, "There remains very much land yet to be possessed" (Joshua 13:1).

Precisely the same challenge confronts us as believers in the New Testament: to move from the legal to the experiential. Like Israel, we must progress one step at a time. Like Israel, too, we will face opposition. Our progress will continually be contested by satanic forces, and we must learn to overcome them with the spiritual weapons God has provided for us. Ultimately, Christ's promises in the New Covenant are given to only one kind of person: "to him who overcomes" (see Revelation 2 and 3). The right to the inheritance is summed up in Revelation 21:7: "He who *overcomes* shall inherit all things" (emphasis added).

To further strengthen and encourage us, God has also set before us the example of Abraham, who is called "the father of us all." Through Abraham, God did not merely establish the measure of the blessings He has prepared for each of us, which is "in all things." He also marked out ahead the path that leads to that blessing. The life of Abraham is both an example and a challenge in three main areas: his prompt obedience, his complete confidence in God's word and his steadfast endurance.

In Hebrews 11:8 the writer emphasizes Abraham's prompt, unquestioning obedience: "By faith Abraham obeyed when he was called to go out to the place which he would receive as an inheritance. And he went out, not knowing where he was going."

Abraham did not ask for any explanation of why he should go, or any description of the place he was going to. He simply did what God told him to do promptly, without questioning. The same kind of obedience characterized his entire life: for instance, when God required him and all his household to be circumcised (see Genesis 17:9–14, 23–27); and even when God asked him to offer up his son Isaac as a sacrifice (see Genesis 22:1–14). At no time did Abraham ever hesitate in his obedience or question God concerning what he was asked to do.

In Romans 4:16–21 Paul points out that when God called Abraham "a father of many nations," he had only one son by Hagar, a slave woman, while Sarah, his wife, had been barren for many years. Yet he reckoned God's description of him as true from the moment it was spoken. Because he thus accepted God's word without questioning, even against the evidence of his own senses, ultimately there came a physical fulfillment that was confirmed by his senses.

Actually, about 25 years passed from the time God first promised Abraham that his descendants would be as numerous as the stars, until the birth of the son who was the promised heir. Through all those years he had nothing to hold onto but God's promise. He must have faced endless temptations to discouragement. Yet he never gave up or abandoned his faith. Finally, the reward of his steadfastness is summed up in Hebrews 6:15: "And so, after he had patiently endured, he obtained the promise."

In Romans 4:11–12 Paul tells us that we are children of Abraham if we "walk in the steps" of Abraham's faith. This is the scriptural requirement for entering into "the blessing of Abraham," promised in Galatians 3:14. Like Abraham, we must accept God's Word as the one sure, unchanging element in our experience. All the variable opinions of men, and all the fluctuating impressions of our senses, are just "grass [that] withers. . . . But the word of our God stands forever" (Isaiah 40:8).

Our acceptance of God's Word, however, must not be purely intellectual or theoretical. We must demonstrate it in our actions just as Abraham did: by prompt, unquestioning obedience and by steadfast endurance in the face of all discouragement. In this way, we shall find that God's Word will ultimately be proved true in our experience. We shall come to know God's blessing—just as Abraham did—"in all things."

Satan will continually oppose us with mental and emotional pressures: doubts, fear, guilt, confusion and so on. He may also assail our bodies with various forms of physical infirmity. Against all this God has provided us with one supremely effective weapon: His Word. In Ephesians 6:17 Paul directs us: "Take . . . the sword of the Spirit, which is the word of God."

This requires the interplay of the human and the divine. The sword is the sword of the Holy Spirit, but it is our responsibility to "take" it. If we take it, the Holy Spirit will wield it. But if we do not take it, the Holy Spirit has nothing to wield.

The Greek word Paul uses here to describe God's Word is *rhema*. This is primarily "a word that is spoken." It becomes effective only when it is spoken through believing lips. It is not the Bible in our bookshelves, or even on our nightstands, that Paul is speaking about. It is the Bible when we take it on our lips *and speak it out with bold faith*.

Our great pattern in the use of this sword is the Lord Jesus Himself, as He demonstrated in His temptation by Satan in the wilderness (see Matthew 4:1–11). Each of Satan's three temptations contained the word *if*. In other words, it was aimed to produce *doubt*.

The first two temptations each began with the phrase *"If* You are the Son of God. . ."* (verses 3 and 6, emphasis added). Shortly before, when Jesus was baptized by John in the Jordan, God the Father had publicly declared, "This is My beloved Son, in whom I am well pleased" (Matthew 3:17). Now Satan was tempting Jesus to doubt what the Father had said about Him.

The third temptation also began with *if,* but it was no longer a temptation merely to doubt, but also to direct disobedience: *"If* You will fall down and worship me. . ."* (verse 9, emphasis added). Satan now challenged Jesus to commit the greatest of all sins: the breaking of the first commandment.

The temptations Satan brings against us, as disciples of Jesus, will follow a similar pattern. First, he will tempt us to doubt what God has said about us; to doubt that our sins have been forgiven, that God really loves us, that we have been accepted into God's family as His children, that we have been released from the curse and have entered into the blessing. But always the final thrust of his temptation will be to direct disobedience.

Jesus used only one weapon to defeat Satan: the *rhema*— the spoken Word of God. He countered each temptation with the same phrase: "It is written." Each was a direct quotation from the Scriptures of the Old Testament. Satan has no defense against the Word of God thus quoted directly at him. He has to withdraw, defeated.

In all of this, Jesus is our perfect example. He did not rely on any wisdom or arguments of His own. He used precisely the same weapon God has given to us: the Word of God. Our security depends on following the example of Jesus. We would certainly be foolish to rely on our own wisdom or strength or righteousness. Satan is a thousand times wiser and stronger than we are. He can point to a thousand flaws in our own righteousness. But there is one weapon against which he has no defense: the Word of God spoken in faith.

231

Such, then, is the path that leads us out of the territory overshadowed by curses into the territory that enjoys the sunlight of God's blessings. Its first requirement is determined, unswerving faith, based on the exchange that took place on the cross. Faith of this kind reckons God's promises as effective from the moment they are apprehended. We do not wait for confirmation from the senses. By prompt, unquestioning obedience and patient endurance, we move from our legal rights in Christ into the full, experiential enjoyment of them. We meet all satanic opposition with "the sword of the Spirit": the spoken Word of God.

Questions for the Study

1. What is the purest and simplest expression of faith?
2. Name two things God does not reveal in advance in keeping His promises.
3. What are the three important facts about the promised blessing, according to Galatians 3:13–14?
4. Many Christians do not fully enjoy the guidance and companionship of the Holy Spirit because they fail to realize that He is a _____.
5. What are the three main areas in which the life of Abraham represents both an example and a challenge?
6. What was the one weapon Jesus used to defeat Satan?

Life Application

1. What can you do to cultivate a personal relationship with the Holy Spirit?
2. Have you ever used God's Word to defeat Satan?

Memory Verse

He has delivered us from the power of darkness and conveyed us into the kingdom of the Son of His love.

Colossians 1:13

Faith Response

Father, I thank You and praise You that You have qualified me to share in the inheritance of the saints (see Colossians 1:12).

Answers

1. Giving thanks.
2. The way He will work and the time He will take.
3. It is specific—"the blessing of Abraham." It comes only in Christ Jesus. And it is defined as "the promise of the [Holy] Spirit."
4. Person.
5. His prompt obedience, his complete confidence in God's word and his steadfast endurance.
6. The *rhema* or spoken word of God.

20

Forceful Men Lay Hold of It

When Joshua was commissioned as the leader who would bring Israel into her inheritance in Canaan, he received the same admonition three times: "Be strong and of good courage" (Joshua 1:6, 9, 18). The first two admonitions came from the Lord Himself; the third came from his fellow Israelites. After the third admonition Joshua must surely have understood one thing: Entering into the Promised Land would not be easy!

The same applies to Christians today who set out to appropriate the promised blessings of the New Covenant. God assures us that He will be with us and fulfill all His promises to us. At the same time, He warns us that we will face various forms of opposition, which will test our faith and our commitment.

In Matthew 11:12 Jesus spoke of the Gospel dispensation He had come to initiate: "From the days of John the Baptist until now, the kingdom of heaven has been forcefully advancing, and forceful men lay hold of it" (NIV). In Luke 16:16 He emphasized the same point: "The Law and

235

the Prophets were proclaimed until John. Since that time, the good news of the kingdom of God is being preached, and everyone is forcing his way into it" (NIV).

Clearly the promise of the Kingdom is not for those who merely indulge in wishful thinking or religious talk. It demands "forcefulness"—an attitude of fixed determination that presses ahead regardless of every kind of difficulty or discouragement.

In Acts 14:22 Paul and Barnabas gave a similar warning to a group of new converts: "We must through many tribulations enter the kingdom of God." Any road that bypasses the tribulations will not take us into the Kingdom. Once we have settled this issue in our own minds, then the tribulations will not deter us.

Otto Aguiar is one man who set out to lay hold of God's promises with forceful determination. Otto is a Brazilian who was born with curses over his life that went back many generations. He had also brought further curses upon himself by his own foolishness. Nevertheless, he has finally crossed over from the dark territory of curses to the sunlit land of God's blessings, which is where he now lives.

Otto Aguiar tells his story:

> I was born fifty years ago in Rio de Janeiro, Brazil. My father was a well-known general from mixed European and Indian stock; my mother came from a family of governors and statesmen. Both sides of my family had been in spiritism for generations.
>
> I was the seventh of ten children—a fourteen-pound breech birth. For several years I was accused of almost killing my mother. I was guilt-ridden and withdrawn. I would sit, hiding my head in my arms, reliving the gruesome experience of being dragged out with forceps, and not ready to cope. I repeated first grade *four* times. By the time I was promoted to second grade, I was almost the size of my teacher.

236

Ancestral curses began to affect the older members of my family while I was still a child. My eldest sister, while in a strict Catholic school, was taken to a spiritist center, and began to "receive spirits of saints," as they say in Brazil. She has spent most of her life in mental institutions.

The second child, my eldest brother, a brilliant student, took a fall on his head at age ten, and became an epileptic. In Brazil at that time it was commonly believed that epilepsy was contagious, so he was moved, with all his belongings, from the main house to the servants' quarters. When he would have an attack, my mother would become totally distraught and scream, "There is no God!" He has been institutionalized for the past fifteen years.

When I was sixteen I began to have all the symptoms of epilepsy—foaming at the mouth, fainting, vomiting, in complete confusion. Yet brain scans showed nothing.

My father, an excellent leader of men, was extremely passive with his seven sons, and exercised no real authority. I cannot remember his even speaking to me until I became a man—yet I adored him. He frequented a spiritist center. I never felt good about spiritism, but would on occasion go myself.

I don't really understand how it happened, but I was accepted for study at a fine arts school—where I obtained a master's degree, with honors in graphic arts! But I never pursued that career. I chose to become a fashion model, and traveled from Brazil to Paris, modeling.

I was heavily involved in drugs and a fast-paced lifestyle. Sometimes I would spend time alone at my family's beach house. I would look at the sky and think of the One who put the stars in the sky and caused the sun to rise. I hungered to know who He was, but I didn't know where to look.

Then I met Ellen, a Jewess from the USA, also a fashion model. When I met her, I decided to change my lifestyle, but I couldn't do it. She went away for five days on an assignment, and I went to the beach with my friends. We were high on drugs and when I entered the rough water, I was immediately dragged in by a powerful wave. Wave after wave slammed on me. I couldn't get my breath. I thought,

O God, now that I've met Ellen and I want to change, am I going to die? This was the first time in my 37 years that I had called on God, but He heard me—and suddenly I was on the sand, trembling and bruised all over, in total panic, yet amazed to be alive.

Within eleven months I not only had a wife, but also a baby—and I could not cope. Instead of hiding my head in my arms as I did as a small boy, I would "phase out" and stare at the ceiling in a trance. . . . I was still a model, and everything else I tried failed . . . so I decided to take my wife and son to Fort Lauderdale, Florida.

My first job was working part-time in a men's clothing shop on fashionable Las Olas Boulevard. I was terrified—I couldn't speak proper English—so I also dug ditches, cracked holes in cement, cleaned bathrooms and washed cars. I had a serious problem with pornography and was in total depression. I could not adjust to American culture, and most of the people I worked for cheated me or didn't pay me at all.

Then we were invited to Good News Church; Ellen was brought to her knees and received the Lord with no intellectual understanding—just fear and trembling! I went forward for salvation the next week, but nothing seemed to happen. The trances got worse; I couldn't keep a job for even one week; my depression was worse; Ellen and I fought constantly because we had no money.

Since Ellen had been involved in the occult, she knew she needed deliverance—and she got it when she renounced everything occult. I could not believe that I needed deliverance from evil spirits—and I also could not believe that God wanted to bless me the way I saw Him blessing others.

By this time, I had done almost every menial task a general's son would never do! People would say, "Why don't you use your creative abilities?" But I was afraid—anything good seemed unattainable.

I went to Derek Prince's seminar on "Curses: Cause and Cure," but nothing happened. I got the tapes and played them over and over. I could see my need, and I desperately wanted to be set free—but it seemed that it didn't work for me.

I got delivered gradually. After two and a half years as a Christian, with no progress, I decided to fast and ask God to help me and deliver me. I was able to fast ten days, and when some Christian friends prayed for me, I received partial deliverance.

For the first time in my life I had some JOY . . . but it didn't last. We had numerous car accidents; I was never able to support my family; I worried about my father in Brazil, who was dying, but we could not possibly afford to go to visit him.

People who tried to help me thought my situation was impossible—I was so passive. I was very uncomfortable with Christian men. . . .

Ellen and two friends began to meet and pray for their husbands at 6:00 A.M. at the prayer house. She would say, "I'm going to pray that you will be a success in all that you put your hand to, and that the Lord will give you a job that you'll love and use the gifts He's set within you." I could not believe that God would answer such a prayer; how could she? (Since then all three women have seen their prayers answered: One husband is now in full-time ministry, one was delivered from alcoholism and I got exactly what my wife prayed for.)

Finally, after six years as a Christian, I went to the pastor for deliverance from evil spirits (after years of being too proud to admit I needed it). Then I went to "Evangelism Explosion" training. When I discovered what Jesus Christ had done for me, I was totally amazed. I had so much JOY—I was in love with God—my co-workers and clients in the store began to come to church to find out what had happened to me!

Again, after a while, my joy dwindled—my job, my finances, my concern for my dying father . . . I was still passive, still frustrated. I began to get an urge to paint—but I was so scared, so afraid of failing. Finally I tried—and I did such primary work that people thought my son, age eight, had done it! But God was stirring up ideas—I began to create in my mind. . . .

239

I decided to go on a forty-day fast. I felt God wanted me to leave my job in the clothing store, but I wanted to be *sure*. I said I wouldn't eat until He spoke to me. After forty days I still had heard nothing. So I ate for two weeks and fasted for two weeks all summer. That was the hardest summer of my life. It was so hard that I learned to *cry out* to God for His mercy. I *begged* Him to speak to me. *I needed to know His will.* My wife and my children would lay hands on me and pray that God would do a miracle in my life. . . .

Then an artist friend gave me some canvas stretched on boards. . . . One Sunday I sent my family to church, and did my first painting.

Two days later, seated in the clothing shop, the Lord spoke to me: *Otto, do you believe that I really want to bless you?*

I said, "Yes, Lord. . . ."

Then why are you sitting here? You are here because you do not want to be blessed. It is your choice. You have never really trusted Me to completely control your life.

I said, "Take it! My life is Yours."

He said, *Take your bag and go home.* (For me, it was as if He had said, "Take up your pallet and walk.")

I got up, walked out and never looked back.

That first painting sold within one week for $80. Within two weeks I was paid $900 for six paintings. After two months my paintings brought $600 each; within one year $1,000; before two years up to $6,500.

I have sold everything I have ever painted and I cannot keep up with the demand—and *I love my work*!

After nine months of painting, not only was I able to support my family, but we had enough money to go to Brazil. My father had *never* heard the Gospel, but when he heard, he believed! I had the joy of seeing my 89-year-old father gather up every ounce of strength to pray the sinner's prayer, and I also led several of my brothers and sisters, plus nurses and strangers, to the Lord. Two weeks after we returned to the U.S., my father died with joy on his face! What a privilege gave me.

240

The main changes in my life seem obviously financial—but, far more important, God completed the revelation of what Jesus did for me on the cross. Now I fully believe He set us free from the curse and that His desire is to bless us, and that He wants us to give Him *complete* control over all that concerns us. That without His power, His grace, I cannot do anything—much less create. I am totally dependent upon His anointing. I *know that He loves me!*

God now speaks to me in dreams and very clearly. . . . I am confident if He wants me to stop painting, it will be to do something better. I'll continue praising Him and trusting.

I now have three precious, healthy children, a happy marriage, wonderful friends and consider myself blessed among men. *I have seen the enemy completely defeated in my own life*, and God has given me a testimony that has encouraged multitudes of Christians and baffled the unsaved.

Otto's story contains a number of features that are typical of people whose lives are overshadowed by curses. It can also encourage those who are seeking to help loved ones in a similar condition. Here are some of the main lessons to be learned.

The root cause of the curses over Otto's life was his ancestors' deep involvement in spiritism over many generations. It has been my observation that curses follow this type of involvement as surely as night follows day.

The ensuing curses did not just affect Otto as an individual. They affected almost all his brothers and sisters, but in various ways. He states that two of them have spent long periods in psychiatric institutions.

One of the first steps in Otto's release was a *correct diagnosis* of his condition. Once he understood clearly that his life was under a curse, he was motivated to seek the release that Jesus had purchased for him through the exchange on the cross.

But, like many others, Otto had lived so long under a curse that he could not envisage God's blessing as a reality in his own life. Left to himself, he probably would never have been able to enter into the blessing. He was too timid and withdrawn. He lacked the "forcefulness" needed to press into God's Kingdom. But persistent intercession by Otto's wife and children, and by others, gradually released him from his timidity and built up in him the determined faith that enabled him to pass from the curse to the blessing.

This should encourage other Christians who are concerned about family members or other loved ones under a curse. Patient, persistent intercession—motivated by love—can release those who are not able to exercise faith for themselves.

Perhaps parents are reading this who realize with deep anguish that their trespassing into the occult has brought curses upon their children, causing them to become captives of Satan. For such parents who repent and seek God with their whole hearts, He has a special promise in Isaiah 49:24–25:

> Can plunder be taken from warriors, or captives rescued from the fierce? But this is what the LORD says: "Yes, captives will be taken from warriors, and plunder retrieved from the fierce; I will contend with those who contend with you, and your children I will save."
>
> NIV

Finally, it is encouraging to look at the extent of the blessings Otto now enjoys. God has blessed him—just as He blessed Abraham—"in all things."

Questions for the Study

1. What was the admonition Joshua received three times when he was commissioned to be Israel's new leader?
2. True or false: If you are walking with the Lord, you will not experience tribulation.
3. What was one of the first steps in Otto's release of the condition of his life?
4. True or false: For many who have lived a long time under a curse, it is hard to envision God's blessing as a reality in their own lives.
5. _____ and _____ intercession that is motivated by love can help family members find release from curses.

Life Application

1. How does Otto's story encourage you to persevere?
2. Do you believe God wants to bless you? If not, why not?

Memory Verse

"Have I not commanded you? Be strong and of good courage; do not be afraid, nor be dismayed."

Joshua 1:9

Faith Response

Lord, I will press on to take hold of that for which You took hold of me (see Philippians 3:12).

Answers

1. "Be strong and of good courage."
2. False. Acts 14:22 states, "We must through many tribulations enter the kingdom of God."
3. Correct diagnosis of the curse.
4. True.
5. Patient, persistent.

21

Beyond Confession: Proclamation, Thanksgiving, Praise

In the prayer of release in chapter 18, the initial focus was on the truth revealed in Hebrews 3:1: Jesus is the "High Priest of our confession." This principle should also govern our ongoing relationship with the Lord. In every situation we encounter, we must respond with an appropriate scriptural confession in order to invoke on our behalf the continuing ministry of Jesus as our High Priest.

In most situations we have three possibilities: to make a positive, scriptural confession; to make no confession; to make a negative, unscriptural confession. If we make a positive confession, we release the ministry of Jesus to help us and to meet our need. If we make no confession, we are left at the mercy of our circumstances. If we make a negative confession, we expose ourselves to evil, demonic forces. In chapter 12, on the theme of "self-imposed curses," various examples were given, showing how negative words release evil and negative forces into people's lives.

It is important to distinguish between the scriptural confession of genuine faith and such things as wishful thinking or irreverent presumption or some kind of "mind-over-matter" philosophy. There are three main differences. First of all, "confession" in the biblical sense is limited to the statements and promises of the Bible. It consists in saying with our mouth what God has already said in His Word. Beyond this confession cannot go.

Second, confession is also limited by the conditions attached to any particular promises. The great majority of the promises in the Bible are *conditional*. God says, in effect, "If you will do this, then I will do that." If we have not done the appropriate "this," then we have no right to expect that God will do the corresponding "that." Confession is valid only if the appropriate conditions have been fulfilled. It is never a substitute for obedience.

Third, confession cannot be reduced to a convenient "system," operated by human will. According to Romans 10:10, confession is effective only if it proceeds from faith in the *heart*. There is a radical difference between faith in the heart and faith in the mind. Faith in the mind is produced by our own mental processes; all it can produce is words, devoid of power. On the other hand, faith in the heart is produced only by the Holy Spirit, and it produces *words charged with power* to accomplish what is confessed. What God has promised to faith in the heart is out of the reach of mere mental faith.

In imparting faith to the heart, the Holy Spirit jealously guards His own sovereignty. He is not amenable to "witchcraft." No one can manipulate Him or intimidate Him or make Him do anything contrary to His own will. Concerning this kind of faith, Paul tells us in Ephesians 2:8–9 that it is "not of yourselves; it is the gift of God, not of works, *lest anyone should boast*" (emphasis added). Mental faith often tends to be boastful and self-assertive. Genuine faith in the heart, on the other hand, humbly acknowledges its total dependence upon God.

With these qualifications, however, confession—rightly understood and practiced—can be a decisive factor in the Christian life. In James 3:4–5 the apostle compares the tongue to the rudder of a ship. Although tiny in comparison to the whole structure of the ship, the rudder determines the course that the ship will follow. Used rightly, it will guide the ship safely to its appointed harbor. Used wrongly, it will cause shipwreck.

This applies to the way we express our faith. Right confession can bring us into all the blessings God has promised. Wrong confession can take us further and further away—into perilous, uncharted seas where some kind of shipwreck awaits us.

People are often unwilling to accept responsibility for the words they speak. According to Jesus, however, there is no way to escape the issue: "For by your words you will be justified, and by your words you will be condemned" (Matthew 12:37). Our words will either confirm our righteousness in God's sight, or they will bring us under condemnation. There is no middle ground.

According to Romans 10:10, faith in the heart becomes fully effective only when it is confessed with the mouth. This is also true of unbelief. When we express our unbelief in words, we release its negative power to work against us, and to withhold from us the blessings God has promised to faith.

The writer of Hebrews offers two further warnings concerning the importance of right confession. In Hebrews 4:14: "Seeing then that we have a great High Priest who has passed through the heavens, Jesus the Son of God, let us hold fast our confession."

Again, in Hebrews 10:21, 23: "And having a High Priest over the house of God . . . let us hold fast the confession of our hope without wavering, for He who promised is faithful."

In each of these passages, there is a direct link between our confession and the ministry of Jesus as our

High Priest. The same principle holds true throughout the New Testament: It is our confession that unites us to Jesus as our High Priest and releases His priestly ministry on our behalf.

The other main emphasis in these passages is on the words *hold fast*. It is important to make the right initial confession, but that is not sufficient by itself. In every subsequent situation where the same issues apply, we must consistently reaffirm our original confession.

In Hebrews 10:23 the writer challenges us not merely to hold fast our confession, but to hold it fast *without wavering*. Clearly he envisages various possible situations that might cause us to waver. "Wavering" might express itself in failing to maintain the initial right confession, or even in changing a positive confession to a negative one. In any case, the warning against wavering indicates that the pressures directed against us all have one objective: to make us retract, or even deny, our original right confession.

The concept of right confession seems so simple, perhaps even simplistic: just to say concerning each problem or each test exactly, and only, what the Bible says about it, and to keep on saying it. Yes, it is simple, but it is not easy! In fact, I have concluded—both from experience in my own life and from observation in the lives of others—that it is perhaps the most searching test of Christian character and commitment.

It is the test that has confronted every martyr. Faced by accusation, threats, torture, he has one supreme commitment: to maintain his confession of the truth *to the end*.

When the accusations come from visible, human enemies, the issues at least are clear. But there is another kind of test, less easy to discern, in which the accusations are inward, directed against the mind by invisible demonic powers. Yet the issue is the same: to maintain the confession of the truth with unwavering determination until those invisible forces are silenced and routed.

Any Christian who successfully passes this test can be assured that he will be an overcomer and that, as such, he will inherit the blessings that God has promised to those who overcome.

To give full, victorious expression to faith, however, there is one further biblical concept that takes us beyond confession. It is "proclamation." Derived from a Latin verb meaning to "shout forth" or to "shout aloud," *proclamation* suggests strong, confident assertion of faith, which cannot be silenced by any form of opposition or discouragement. It implies a transition from a defensive posture to one of *attack*.

In Psalm 118:11–17 the psalmist describes such an experience. His enemies had surrounded him on every side and were about to destroy him, but the Lord intervened and gave him victory. His transition from defense to attack is described in verses 15 and 17: "Shouts of joy and victory resound in the tents of the righteous: 'The LORD's right hand has done mighty things!' . . . I will not die but live, and will *proclaim* what the LORD has done" (NIV, emphasis added).

It was the psalmist's joyful, confident proclamation of what the Lord had done for him that set the seal on his victory. Rightly practiced, it will do the same for us.

As we practice the confident proclamation of all that God has provided for us through the sacrifice of Jesus, it will naturally lead us on to two further forms of expression: thanksgiving and praise. If we truly believe what we proclaim, this is the only appropriate response! Wherever there is genuine faith, proclamation will always be followed by thanksgiving and praise.

Although thanksgiving and praise are closely related, there is a distinction between them. Simply stated, we thank God for what He *does*; we praise Him for who He *is*. Joined together, thanksgiving and praise give us direct access to God's presence.

This is depicted vividly in the imagery of Psalm 100:4: "Enter into His gates with thanksgiving, and into His courts with praise. Be thankful to Him, and bless His name."

The psalmist pictures two stages in approaching God. First, we enter His *gates* with *thanksgiving*; then, we pass through His *courts* with *praise*. This brings us into the immediate presence of God. If we do not fulfill these requirements for access, we can still cry out to God—but only from a distance. In His mercy He will respond to our cry, but we have no direct access into His presence.

Thanksgiving and praise are the two most immediate ways in which our faith can respond to God. Whenever God gives us a promise of blessing or reveals a provision He has made for us, we need to respond like Abraham and accept God's word to us as true from the moment it is spoken. Logically, therefore, we begin to thank and praise Him immediately. We do not wait until we have actually experienced the fulfillment of the promise or the provision.

In 2 Chronicles 20, this principle is illustrated by an event in the reign of Jehoshaphat, king of Judah. Word had come to the king that a vast invading army was advancing against him from the south. Jehoshaphat knew that he did not have the military resources to oppose this army. Consequently, he summoned all his people together to seek God's help by united prayer and fasting.

God responded to their prayer by a prophetic utterance, given through a Levite, which directed Jehoshaphat to lead his people against the enemy by a certain route. It also contained words of assurance and encouragement:

> "Do not be afraid nor dismayed because of this great multitude, for the battle is not yours, but God's. . . . You will not need to fight in this battle. Position yourselves, stand still and see the salvation of the LORD, who is with you."
>
> 2 Chronicles 20:15, 17

Nothing had changed at this point in the military situation, but Jehoshaphat received God's promise *by faith*, without demanding further evidence. The next day

> he appointed those who should sing to the LORD, and who should praise the beauty of holiness, as they went out before the army and were saying: "Praise the LORD, for His mercy endures forever."
>
> 2 Chronicles 20:21

This was certainly not the conventional way for an army to go into battle—but it worked! As soon as the Lord heard the praises of His people, He intervened sovereignly and supernaturally by sending a spirit of division among the various national groups within the invading army. Suddenly, and for no apparent reason, they began to fight each other, until all were totally destroyed. The people of Judah did not need to fight, but only to gather the booty from their slain enemies! God intervened in this way because His people responded to His promises by faith, without waiting for further confirmation.

Two important principles are illustrated by this account. First, God expects us to praise Him for the promises He gives us, without waiting to see them fulfilled. Second, praise offered in faith releases the supernatural intervention of God on our behalf. Briefly stated: Faith begins to praise God *before* the promised victory, not merely after it.

In the New Testament, in Acts 16, the experience of Paul and Silas in Philippi dramatically illustrates the same principles. As a result of casting a demon out of a slave girl, they had been unjustly arrested, savagely abused and beaten, and then thrown into the maximum security section of the jail, with their feet in stocks. There was no ray of light in their darkness, no source of comfort or encouragement in their physical situation, no assurance as to what the future held.

Yet in their spirits they knew that nothing could change the eternal faithfulness of God, and nothing could rob them of the victory Christ had won for them. The logic of their faith triumphed over the logic of their circumstances. At midnight—the darkest hour—they were singing hymns of praise to God!

Their praises did the same for them as for Jehoshaphat's army: They released the supernatural intervention of God on their behalf. "Suddenly there was a great earthquake, so that the foundations of the prison were shaken; and immediately all the doors were opened and everyone's chains were loosed" (Acts 16:26).

The lesson of Jehoshaphat's army and of Paul and Silas in the jail is summed up by the Lord Himself in Psalm 50:23: "He who sacrifices thank offerings honors me, and he prepares the way so that I may show him the salvation of God" (NIV).

God's salvation is already complete through the sacrifice of Jesus on the cross. Nothing we say or do can ever change that. But when we respond with sacrifices of thanksgiving and praise, we open the way for salvation's benefits to be manifested in our lives. Like Jehoshaphat, and like Paul and Silas, we must learn to offer these sacrifices in faith, before we have actually experienced the benefits.

In Psalm 20:5 David said, "In the name of our God we will set up our banners!" Again, in Song of Solomon 6:10, the Bride of Christ is portrayed as "awesome as an army with banners." Three of the most effective "banners" God has given us are *proclamation*, *thanksgiving* and *praise*.

First, we raise the banner of *proclamation*. We speak out boldly, in faith, the promise or the provision of God's Word that applies to our particular situation or meets our particular need. Then we go on to thank God—still in faith—for the truth we have proclaimed. Finally, we move from *thanksgiving* to the jubilant *praise*. All this we do *in pure faith*, without waiting for any visible change in our situation.

252

In His own way and time, God responds to our faith, just as He did to that of Abraham. The truth, which we have proclaimed and for which we have thanked and praised Him, becomes a reality in our experience.

By raising these three banners of proclamation, thanksgiving and praise, we achieve two purposes at one and the same time. First, we secure for ourselves the promised blessings of God that we have proclaimed. Second, we shut out the satanic forces that would resist us and seek to withhold the blessings from us. In this way, marching together into our inheritance, we fulfill Solomon's prophetic picture of an army awesome with banners.

Questions for the Study

1. What principle should govern our ongoing relationship with the Lord?
2. What are the three possibilities open to us regarding our confession?
3. Confession in the biblical sense is limited to the _____ and _____ of the Bible.
4. True or false: The great majority of promises in the Bible are conditional.
5. According to Romans 10:10, faith in the heart becomes fully effective only when it is _____ by the mouth.
6. Where there is genuine faith, proclamation will always be followed by _____ and _____.
7. What two principles are illustrated by the story of the worshipers who preceded Jehoshaphat's army?

Life Application

1. Are proclamation, thanksgiving and praise a daily part of your spiritual life? If not, why not?
2. What can you do to make these activities more active in your life?

Memory Verse

"He who sacrifices thank offerings honors me, and he prepares the way so that I may show him the salvation of God."

Psalm 50:23, NIV

Faith Response —————————————————————

Almighty God, like King David I declare that "I will praise You, O LORD, with my whole heart; I will tell of all Your marvelous works" (Psalm 9:1).

Answers

1. That Jesus is the "High Priest of our confession" (Hebrews 3:1).
2. To make a positive, scriptural confession; to make no confession; and to make a negative, unscriptural confession.
3. Statements, promises.
4. True.
5. Confessed.
6. Thanksgiving, praise.
7. Faith praises God before the promised victory; and praise offered in faith releases God's victory.

22

Proclamations for Continuing Victory

The truths I have been sharing in this book are much more than the outcome of an intellectual pursuit of knowledge in the abstract. On the contrary, I have "mined" them out of intense, persistent prayer and spiritual conflict, in which Ruth and I have shared together for at least three years. Every main truth unfolded in this book has been subjected first to the test of our own experience. I have not felt free to pass on to others theories that have not worked for us.

In the previous chapter I explained how proclamation, thanksgiving and praise, working together, can release into our lives the promised blessings of God. In this chapter I am going to share briefly how Ruth and I have been learning to apply this principle in our own lives. The regular practice of proclaiming God's Word, and then thanking and praising Him for it, has become an integral part of our personal spiritual discipline. We regard this as one of the most valuable truths that God has opened to us from the Scriptures.

God has led us to establish a central "bank" of Scriptures, which we have memorized and which we draw upon in our times of prayer, or whenever we become involved in spiritual conflict. Proclaiming these in faith invariably releases corresponding expressions of thanksgiving and praise.

Normally, we speak these out loud, alone or together. We are not talking to one another, however, nor to the walls or the ceiling of our room. We are speaking to a vast, invisible world of spirit beings: first of all, to God the Father, the Son and the Spirit; then to all the heavenly beings who worship and serve God, and who have been appointed "ministering spirits, sent out to render service for the sake of those who will inherit salvation" (Hebrews 1:14, NASB). We are also conscious that we are surrounded by a "great cloud of witnesses," made up of the saints of all ages who have victoriously completed their earthly pilgrimage (see Hebrews 12:1, NIV).

We believe that this is a legitimate application of Hebrews 12:22–24:

> But you have come to Mount Zion, to the heavenly Jerusalem, the city of the living God. You have come to thousands upon thousands of angels in joyful assembly, to the church of the firstborn, whose names are written in heaven. You have come to God, the judge of all men, to the spirits of righteous men made perfect, to Jesus the mediator of a new covenant, and to the sprinkled blood that speaks a better word than the blood of Abel.
>
> NIV

Also included in our audience, however, are Satan and all the evil angels and other demonic beings under his control. These operate in a way exactly opposite to God's ministering angels. Their purpose is to inflict every form of harm and evil on the entire human race, but first and foremost on those who are serving the true God.

In this context, our proclamation has two effects. On the one hand, it invokes on our behalf the help of God and His angels. On the other hand, it protects us from the schemes and assaults of Satan and his demonic forces.

This form of proclamation is continually building up our faith. According to Romans 10:17, "Faith comes by hearing . . . the word [the *rhema*, the spoken word] of God." Hearing others speak God's Word is helpful, but hearing ourselves speak it is even more effective. As we both speak and hear, both edges of the sword of God's Word are at work in us simultaneously (see Hebrews 4:12).

Finally, when we make the same proclamation together, in harmony, supernatural power is released. Jesus says, "If two of you agree [harmonize] . . . concerning anything . . . it will be done for them by My Father in heaven" (Matthew 18:19). The power of one believer making a proclamation on his own is tremendous, but the power of two or more making the same proclamation together in harmony increases by geometric progression.

There are many times and situations, of course, when it would be out of place to make a proclamation out loud. The alternative is to make the same proclamation inaudibly in one's mind. Inaudible words can also make a powerful impact in the spiritual realm.

This is probably the most effective way to deal with lies and accusations with which the enemy bombards our minds. The mind is the main field of battle in all conflicts of this kind. When our minds are actively responding to the Word we are proclaiming inwardly, no room is left for the enemy's negative thoughts and insinuations.

In all of this, however, we must be careful to recognize our continuing dependency on the Holy Spirit. Otherwise, the carnal mind can reduce these principles to a "system" in which God plays the role of a "heavenly vending machine." We simply insert the right proclamation, and out comes any brand of carnal gratification that we select! Obviously, this is a caricature of a believer's relationship with God.

There may be a wide gap between the way we view ourselves and the way the Holy Spirit views us. We may be conscious of what we *want*, whereas the Holy Spirit sees what we *need*. He alone can be trusted to direct each of us to the type of proclamation that applies to our individual situation and level of faith. In this way, God can accomplish His purpose in our lives.

With this caution, I feel it would be helpful for me to list on the following pages, simply as patterns, some of the proclamations that Ruth and I make regularly, together with the situations in which they would be appropriate. So far as possible, we "personalize" the Scriptures we quote. For instance, if a statement is addressed to believers and introduced with the pronoun "you," we normally change it to "I" or "we," and also make any other grammatical changes that are indicated.

My list opens with Scriptures that are directly connected with the theme of this book, but continues with others that have a more general application. Some comments and words of explanation are interspersed. In each case, the relevant Scripture reference is given.

1. As a result of praying the prayer of release from curses (see chapter 18)

Through the sacrifice of Jesus on the cross, I have passed out from under the curse and entered into the blessing of Abraham, whom God blessed in all things.

based on Galatians 3:13–14

Ruth has received release from many curses over her life, but she has had a continuing battle walking it out in experience. This proclamation has therefore become particularly significant for us. We often make it several times in a day. Over the past two or three years we have repeated these words many hundreds of times. Each time we do so, we move further away from effects of curses and into the blessing that is our inheritance.

2. When becoming aware of negative forces directed against us, either from servants of Satan or from soulish utterances of Christians (see chapters 13, 14 and 15)

No weapon formed against me shall prosper, and every tongue that rises against me in judgment I do now condemn. This is my heritage [my inheritance right] as a servant of the LORD, and my righteousness is from You, O LORD.

based on Isaiah 54:17

There are two important points to note in connection with this proclamation. First, we are not directed to ask God to condemn any tongue that speaks against us. God has given us the authority to do this for ourselves, and He expects us to exercise it.

Second, our right to exercise this authority depends on the fact that we are not acting out of our own righteousness, but because God's righteousness is imputed to us on the basis of our faith. Clearly this proceeds out of the exchange by which Jesus, on the cross, was made sin with our sinfulness that we might become righteous with His righteousness. The various benefits of that exchange are all interrelated, and should not be separated from each other.

But God requires more of us than just turning back the evil words spoken against us. After that, He instructs us to forgive those who seek to harm us. Finally, He expects us to move from the negative to the positive: to respond to a curse with a blessing.[1]

Blessing those who curse us, just like forgiving those who harm us, does not depend on our emotions. It proceeds from a firm decision of our will, made in obedience to God's Word. Here is a suitable form of words that covers both forgiving and blessing:

> Lord, I forgive all who have spoken evil against me, and having forgiven them, I bless them in Your name.

Altogether, we need to follow three successive steps in responding to those who curse us. First, we condemn the tongue that has uttered the curse. Second, we forgive the person from whom the curse proceeded. Third, we ask God to bless the person. By carrying out these three steps, we can dissipate any spiritual darkness or heaviness that a curse has brought on us.

3. When pressures of sin or guilt or unworthiness pursue us from our past

> I am in Christ, and therefore I am a new creation. All those old things have passed away. Everything in my life has become new, and everything is from God.
>
> based on 2 Corinthians 5:17–18

God accepts total responsibility for the new creation. It is all His doing. Nothing is carried over from the old creation, which has been marred and corrupted by sin.

When the past reasserts its claims over us, we need to meditate on the picture John gives us in Revelation 21:5:

> Then He who sat on the throne said, "Behold, I make all things new." And He said to me, "Write, for these words are true and faithful."

These words come from the One who sits on the throne, the One who has under His control the entire universe and everything in it. That includes every detail of our lives. He reaffirms that He makes *everything* new.

It seems that John might have wondered inwardly whether this was too stupendous a claim, even for God. But the Lord assures him: "Write, for these words are true and faithful." It is as if He says: "Yes, John, you really can assure My people: I do exactly what I say."

4. When oppressed by hopelessness and gloomy forebodings of death

I will not die but live, and will proclaim what the LORD has done.

Psalm 118:17, NIV

Of course, this does not mean "I will never die"—but only "I will not die before God's appointed time—I will not allow myself to be murdered by Satan." Proclaimed with faith and understanding, this verse can deliver and protect those who are assailed by the spirit of death. It can be used to revoke the negative utterances by which people expose themselves to that spirit. (For examples, see chapter 12.)

For some people it may be necessary to repeat this proclamation many times over, until it becomes more real than all their previous negative thought patterns. Remember that Jesus required Peter to reaffirm his love for Him just as many times as he had previously denied Him.

5. When assailed by physical sickness or infirmity

Jesus Himself bore my sins in His own body on the tree, that I, having died to sins, might live for righteousness—by whose wounds I was healed.

based on 1 Peter 2:24

I have also prepared the following special proclamation, which combines truths from many different Scriptures and which has helped Christians in many areas of the world:

> My body is a temple for the Holy Spirit, redeemed, cleansed and sanctified by the blood of Jesus. My members—the parts of my body—are instruments of righteousness, presented to God for His service and for His glory. The devil has no place in me, no power over me, no unsettled claims against me. All has been settled by the blood of Jesus.
>
> I overcome Satan by the blood of the Lamb and by the word of my testimony, and I do not love my life to the death. My body is for the Lord, and the Lord is for my body.
>
> based on 1 Corinthians 6:19; Ephesians 1:7;
> 1 John 1:7; Hebrews 13:12; Romans 6:13; 8:33–34;
> Revelation 12:11; 1 Corinthians 6:13

Someone might ask, Is it honest for me to make proclamations such as these, when I see in my body the physical evidences of sickness, or when I feel in my soul the oppositions of sins? The answer depends on your point of view. If you are looking at yourself in your own natural condition, then it is not honest. But if you are looking at yourself as God sees you in Christ, then you have the right to make such a proclamation.

Once we have repented of our sins and committed ourselves to Christ, God no longer looks at us as we are in our natural state. Instead, He looks at us from the perspective of the exchange that took place on the cross. Spiritually, He sees us as made righteous; physically, He sees us as made whole.

It is significant that, in the Scriptures, the healing provided through the sacrifice of Jesus is never spoken of in the future tense. In Isaiah 53:5, written more than seven hundred years before the death of Jesus, healing is already presented as an accomplished fact: "By his wounds *we are healed*" (NIV, emphasis added). In the New Testament, in 1 Peter 2:24 (paraphrased above), the apostle refers to

263

Isaiah 53:5, but uses the past tense: "By whose stripes *you were healed*" (emphasis added).

When the words we speak about ourselves agree with what God says about us in Christ, then we open the way for Him to make us in actual experience all that He says we are. But if we fail to make the appropriate confession—or proclamation—about ourselves, we are confined to the prison of our own natural state. We have shut ourselves off from the supernatural, transforming grace of God, which works only through faith.

Again, someone might ask, What about someone who says and does all the right things, and yet the promised results do not follow? An answer is to be found in the words of Moses in Deuteronomy 29:29: "The secret things belong to the LORD our God, but those things which are revealed belong to us and to our children forever, that we may do all the words of this law."

The reason some people do not receive some part of the promised blessings often belongs in the category of "secret things." It is vain for us to seek to pry God's secrets from Him. It is also irreverent. If God withholds an answer, it is more important to trust than to understand.

On the other hand, the words of Moses remind us of our responsibility, as God's people, to believe, to proclaim and to act upon those things He has clearly revealed in His Word. Central to these is the provision God has made for us through the sacrifice of Jesus on the cross. We must not let our concern about the secret things keep us from believing and obeying the things that are revealed.

6. When Satan attacks an area for which God holds us responsible—our home, our family, our business, our ministry, etc.

The bolts of our gates will be iron and bronze, and our strength will equal our days.

There is no one like the God of Jeshurun, who rides on the heavens to help us and on the clouds in His majesty.

The eternal God is our refuge, and underneath are the everlasting arms. He will drive out our enemy before us, saying, "Destroy him!"

based on Deuteronomy 33:25–27, NIV

By this proclamation we are enabled to move from defense to attack. First of all, "our gates" represent our defense system. God promises that this will be strong enough to keep out our enemy's attack. Then there is a wonderful picture of God intervening supernaturally on our behalf: "He rides on the heavens to help us." Our proclamation is one way that we invoke His intervention.

Finally, there is assurance of our enemy's defeat: "He [God] will drive out our enemy before us." God requires us to play our part in this final stage; therefore, He says, "Destroy him!" He has equipped us with the spiritual weapons we need to do this.

7. When we awaken to the realization that the mind is a battlefield in which the lies of Satan are at war with the truths of God's Word

The weapons of my warfare are mighty in God. With them I pull down the strongholds that Satan has built in my mind. I bring all my thoughts into obedience to Christ. Three of my mightiest weapons are proclamation, thanksgiving and praise.

based on 2 Corinthians 10:4–5

It is important to remember, however, that our "enemies" in the Christian life are not our fellow human beings. Our enemies are the vile spiritual forces directed against us from the kingdom of Satan. Paul makes this clear in Ephesians 6:12: "For we are not fighting against people made of flesh and blood, but against persons without bodies—the evil rulers of the unseen world . . . and against huge numbers of wicked spirits in the spirit world" (TLB).

In this strange kind of warfare to which God has called us, the standards of measurement are different from those we use in the world of the senses. Measured by the spiritual scale, *forgiving* is stronger than *resenting*; *blessing* is stronger than *cursing*; *giving thanks* is stronger than *complaining*; *praise* is stronger than *accusation*; and *loving* is stronger than *hating*.

Based on this paradox, here are two proclamations that unlock God's strength and God's enabling when our own resources fail.

8. When confronted by a task too big for me

I can do all things through the One who empowers me within.

based on Philippians 4:13

9. When my own strength fails or is insufficient

God's strength is made perfect in my weakness, and so when I am weak, then I am strong.

based on 2 Corinthians 12:9–10

Finally, here are two proclamations that cover needs that arise at sometime or other in the lives of almost all of us.

10. When exercising faith for financial needs

God is able to make all grace abound toward us, that we, always having all sufficiency in all things, may have an abundance for every good work.

based on 2 Corinthians 9:8

The level of God's provision for His people is revealed as *abundance*, not mere sufficiency. Ruth and I make this proclamation regularly, as the financial base for Derek Prince Ministries.

11. When assailed by fear

God has not given me a spirit of fear, but of power and of love and of a sound mind.

based on 2 Timothy 1:7

In the name of Jesus I submit to God and I resist the spirit of fear. Therefore it has to flee from me.

based on James 4:7

The above Scriptures are only a few examples. There is no limit to the number of scriptural proclamations we can make. Each of us must rely on the Holy Spirit to guide us to those that suit our particular situations.

Choosing and making appropriate proclamations based on Scripture has one very important result. We receive and apply God's Word in the *active*, not the passive mode. We no longer just read a Scripture and then pass on. Instead, we go through three successive stages. First, we ask the Holy Spirit to direct us to Scriptures that are especially appropriate for us. Second, we fix them firmly in our minds. Third, by proclaiming them, we release their power into the areas of our lives where we need them.

Perhaps you are one of the many Christians today who feel the need to "take the sword of the Spirit"—referred to in chapter 19—but do not know of a simple and practical way to do this. If so, Ruth and I would like to recommend to you this method of selective proclamation of Scriptures. We have practiced it in our own lives, and we can say, *It works!*

But let me add one final word of warning! Do not put your faith in your proclamation, or in any other method or procedure. *Our faith must be in God alone*—not in anyone or anything else. Our proclamation is merely an effective way to express the faith we have in God.

So now, as you set your face toward the land of God's blessings, receive the admonition given three times to Joshua:

"Be strong and of good courage!"

Questions for the Study

1. Proclamation has two effects; name them.
2. True or false: Speaking a proclamation inaudibly will not help you.
3. What are the three successive steps needed when responding to those who curse us?
4. In the kind of warfare to which God has called His children, what is stronger than resenting?
5. Making appropriate proclamations indicates that we receive and apply God's Word in the _____, not the passive mode.

Life Application

1. Why is the Holy Spirit's involvement important when you proclaim Scripture?
2. Is memorizing Scripture important? Why or why not?
3. Take the time to proclaim each of the eleven proclamation Scriptures listed on pages 259–67.

Memory Verse

Choose one of the verses in this chapter to memorize.

Faith Response

Lord, I give You thanks for the victory You have given me through Jesus Christ. It is by faith that I overcome (see 1 Corinthians 15:57; 1 John 5:4).

Answers

1. It invokes the help of God and protects us from the schemes and assaults of Satan.
2. False. Inaudible words can make a powerful impact in the spiritual realm.
3. We must (1) condemn the tongue, (2) forgive the person and (3) ask God to bless that person.
4. Forgiving.
5. Active.

Important Afterwords

Introduction

The theme of *blessings* and *curses* is central to the whole of God's dealings with the human race. It can be compared to the trunk of a tree whose branches reach out in many different directions. A systematic study raises important, practical questions about various other main areas of biblical truth.

This section deals with two of these questions:

1. Is it possible at this present time, through faith, to experience release from all the curses that sin has brought upon the human race? If not, when—and how—will this finally be accomplished?
2. The Old Testament contains many examples of God's servants who pronounced curses on His enemies. What should the Christian response be when we are opposed and mistreated?

23

Curses Not Yet Revoked

On the cross Jesus took upon Himself all the evil consequences that disobedience to God had brought upon the
human race. These fall into two main categories: those
brought upon man by his original disobedience in the Garden; and those pronounced later in connection with the
Law given through Moses.

In Galatians 3:13 Paul refers to this latter category. He
states specifically that "Christ has redeemed us from *the
curse of the law*" (emphasis added). He relates this to the
fact that the Law had declared that anyone executed by
hanging on a tree had—by that very fact—become a curse.
The same Law that pronounced the curse thus opened the
way for deliverance from the curse through the substitutionary sacrifice of Christ.

In chapter 4 we summarized "the curse of the Law" as
follows: humiliation; barrenness, unfruitfulness; mental
and physical sickness; family breakdown; poverty; defeat;
oppression; failure; God's disfavor.

According to the clear statement of Paul in Galatians 3:13, the death of Christ on the cross offers deliverance from all these consequences of the broken Law. Paul does not here include, however, the various forms of the original curse that God pronounced upon Adam and Eve after their disobedience in the Garden. This curse—recorded in Genesis 3:16–19—falls into two main sections, the first spoken to Eve, and the second spoken to Adam.

The curse spoken to Eve relates to her unique function as a woman and it again falls into two sections:

1. Childbearing would be arduous and painful.
2. She would be subject to her husband's authority and dependent upon him for the fulfillment of her basic feminine desire for children.

The curse spoken to Adam relates primarily to the original task assigned to him by God in Genesis 2:15 to "tend and [keep the garden]"—that is, to cultivate the soil. This curse can be divided into three main sections:

1. The nature of the soil would undergo a change. Henceforth, it would yield its produce only by hard, sweat-producing labor.
2. The evidence of the change in the soil would be seen in a change in the vegetation it would produce— specifically in the growth of two unproductive forms of vegetation: thorns and thistles.
3. Man himself would be subject to decay and death, doomed ultimately to return to the dust from which he was taken. Though directed to Adam, this third section actually affected Eve as well, together with their descendants.

It is clear that the curses pronounced at this time also affected the earth itself. This followed from the close connection between Adam and his environment, which is indicated by the Hebrew word for "earth": *adamah*. Adam himself was made from the earth. He was also held responsible by God for the care of the earth.

In addition, a special curse was placed upon the serpent, which thereafter distinguished it from all other members of the animal kingdom (see Genesis 3:14–15).

In Ecclesiastes 1:2 and in Romans 8:20, the condition of the earth and its inhabitants produced by these curses is described by two words that have the same meaning: *vanity* and *futility*.

The redemption from "the curse of the law," to which Paul refers in Galatians 3:13, does not include the curses described above. These resulted from the original disobedience of Adam and Eve in the Garden. At this time there was no God-given system of law, and consequently no curse pronounced for breaking it.

In Romans 5:13–14 Paul says: "For until the law sin was in the world, but sin is not imputed when there is no law. Nevertheless death reigned from Adam to Moses, even over those who had not sinned according to the likeness of the transgression of Adam."

During this period "from Adam to Moses," humanity was without any God-given system of law. All men suffered, however, from the effects of the curse pronounced originally upon Adam and Eve, and each person paid the penalty for his own individual sin, which was death.

The beginning of the period of the Law is indicated in John 1:17: "The law was given through Moses." In connection with the giving of the Law, a long series of curses was pronounced on those who came under the Law, but then failed to keep it. These are the curses that are listed primarily in Deuteronomy 28:15–68. Collectively, they are called "the curse of the law." When Paul says in Galatians 3:13 that "Christ has redeemed us from the curse of the law," it is to these curses that he refers.

What about the curses pronounced originally on Adam and Eve? Has God provided redemption also from these? And if so, upon what basis?

To answer these questions, we need to recognize two different ways in which Jesus, when He came to earth, was identified with those whom He came to redeem. The New Testament depicts two different aspects of His identification with humanity, which are indicated by the two different genealogies given for Him.

In Matthew His genealogy is traced back to Abraham (see Matthew 1:1–17). As the promised "seed of Abraham," He identified with Abraham's descendants, the nation of Israel, who were under the Law. In Galatians 4:4–5 Paul says that Jesus was "born under the law, to redeem those who were under the law."

In Luke, however, the genealogy of Jesus is traced back to Adam, and He is thus identified with the whole race descended from Adam (see Luke 3:23–38). During His earthly life the title He applied to Himself more than any other was "Son of man." In Hebrew the name *Adam* is also the word for *man*. Thus, "Son of man" is also "Son of Adam." By using this title, therefore, Jesus continually emphasized His identification with all of Adam's descendants—the whole human race.

Because of this identification, the substitutionary sacrifice of Jesus on the cross did not merely provide redemption from the curse of the broken Law. It also provided deliverance from all the evil consequences that the original sin of Adam had brought upon all his descendants—whether under the Law or not.

This is brought out by two different titles that Paul gives to Jesus in 1 Corinthians 15. In verse 45 he calls Him "the last Adam," and in verse 47 "the second Man." These two titles refer respectively to the death and the resurrection of Jesus.

On the cross Jesus died as "the last Adam." He took upon Himself all the evil consequences that Adam's disobedience had brought upon the entire human race. When He died, they were terminated. When He was buried, they were forever put away.

Then on the third day Jesus rose again from the dead as "the second Man." He thus became the Head of an entirely new race—the Immanuel race, the God-man race—a race in which the nature of God and man are blended together in a new creation.

All those who by faith and commitment are identified with Jesus in His death, His burial and His resurrection become members of this new race. In 1 Peter 1:3–4 the apostle says of these: "God . . . has begotten us again to a living hope through the resurrection of Jesus Christ from the dead, to an inheritance incorruptible and undefiled and that does not fade away."

There were, therefore, two complementary aspects to the redemption from the curse provided through the death of Jesus. As "the seed of Abraham," born under the law, He took upon Himself all the curses of the broken Law summed up in Deuteronomy 28:15–68. As "the last Adam," He also took upon Himself the curses pronounced upon Adam and Eve for their original act of disobedience. As we have seen, these extended also to earth's soil and its vegetation, being specifically manifested in two unproductive forms of vegetation: thorns and thistles.

The New Testament uses very beautiful imagery to reveal how Jesus took upon Himself not merely the curses upon Adam and Eve, but also the curse upon the earth. In John 19:5 the apostle records the scene when Pilate brought Jesus out before His accusers: "Then Jesus came out, wearing the crown of thorns and the purple robe. And Pilate said to them, 'Behold the Man!'"

The phrase *the Man* pointed out Jesus as a descendant of Adam—unique in His perfection, yet representative of the whole race. At the same time, Jesus' attire represented the double curse that Adam had brought upon the earth. The crown on His head represented the curse of *thorns*; the purple color of His robe represented the curse of *thistles*.

This brief but vivid scene revealed Jesus as "the last Adam," who took upon Himself both the curse that had come upon Adam and Eve, and also the curse that their sin had brought upon the earth.

From every point of view, therefore, the redemption from the curse provided by the death of Jesus was complete. It covered every curse that had ever come upon humanity. It covered the curse pronounced upon Adam and Eve for their disobedience; it covered the curse their disobedience had brought upon the earth; and it covered all the curses subsequently pronounced in connection with the Law of Moses.

Further study of Scripture indicates, however, that full redemption from the curse will be worked out in successive phases. Redemption from "the curse of the law" is already offered in this present age to those who can appropriate it by faith. It will be manifested in its completeness only upon the return of Christ. At that time, too, those who are caught up to meet Him will finally and forever be released from the Adamic curse.

In Philippians 3:20–21 Paul describes the change that will take place at this time in the body of each redeemed believer:

> For our citizenship is in heaven, from which we also eagerly wait for the Savior, the Lord Jesus Christ, who will transform our lowly body that it may be conformed to His glorious body, according to the working by which He is able even to subdue all things to Himself.

Paul here contrasts two kinds of bodies: "our lowly body" and "His [Christ's] glorious body." More literally, these phrases could be rendered "the body of our humiliation" and "the body of His glory." The curse pronounced upon Adam confined him—and his descendants—in "a body of humiliation." As such, it reminds each of us continually of our fallen condition.

From the moment of birth, this body is continually subject to decay, depending on many external factors for life and well-being. By luxury and self-indulgence we may briefly seek to forget our inherent weaknesses, yet within a matter of moments we are inevitably confronted once more with our body's humiliating limitations.

We may put on the most elegant and expensive clothes, but as soon as we become physically active, the smell of our sweat reminds us that we are confined in "a body of humiliation." Or we may fill our stomachs with the finest of food and drink. Within a few hours, however, we will be compelled to empty our bladders and our bowels—actions that leave no room for pomp or arrogance.

For those who have accepted the redemption provided by Christ, all these humiliating features of our present body will be changed not gradually or progressively, but in one single, glorious moment. In 1 Corinthians 15:51–53 Paul describes this supernatural transformation:

> We shall not all sleep [in death], but we shall all be changed—in a moment, in the twinkling of an eye, at the last trumpet. For the trumpet will sound, and the dead will be raised incorruptible, and we shall be changed. For this corruptible must put on incorruption, and this mortal must put on immortality.

Altogether, in 1 Corinthians 15, Paul sums up the following five changes that will take place in the body of each believer at the return of Christ:

1. From corruptible to incorruptible
2. From mortal to immortal

279

3. From dishonor to glory
4. From weakness to power
5. From natural—literally, "soulish"—to spiritual

All the five negative features in the above list are the effects of the original curse on Adam. Full deliverance from all of them will come first to the believers who are caught up to meet Christ at His return. In James 1:18 these are described as "a kind of firstfruits of [God's] creatures." The transformation they undergo will serve as a guarantee of the redemption that will ultimately come to the whole creation.

In the period that will follow for earth's remaining inhabitants, the righteousness and justice of Christ's millennial reign will minimize, but not abolish, the curse of the Law. Human life will be greatly extended, but the Adamic curse also will still prevail. Earth, too, as well as the animal creation, will experience a period of fruitfulness and abundance without parallel since the Fall—but "futility" will not yet be done away with. The full and final abolition of every curse must wait until the period of "new heavens and a new earth" (2 Peter 3:13).

All this will be the outworking of the exchange by which Jesus on the cross was made a curse in order to cancel every curse that man's disobedience had brought on himself and on creation. In Revelation 22:3 its consummation is summed up in one brief, but comprehensive, statement: "And there shall be no more curse."

Questions for the Study

1. Name the two main curses that Jesus redeemed us from. *the Law; Adam's curse*
2. The original curse pronounced on Adam related primarily to what assigned task? *tend the garden*
3. True or false: The redemption Jesus bought by His sacrifice on the cross covered both the curse of the Law and the evil consequences of Adam's original sin. *T*
4. When Jesus arose from the dead on the third day as "the second Man," He became the Head of what new race? *Immanuel race; God-man race*
5. When Pilate brought Jesus before His accusers, Jesus' crown and His robe represented two aspects of the original curse. What were they? *thorn & thistle*
6. True or false: The full and final abolition of every curse will occur during Jesus' millennial reign. *F*

Life Application

1. How does knowing about the curses that are not yet revoked help you in your Christian walk?
2. In 1 Corinthians 15 Paul tells us about the changes that will occur at Christ's return. What impact does knowing this have on your faith and life in Christ now?

Memory Verse

Choose another verse from chapter 22 to memorize.

Faith Response

Thank You, Jesus, that my citizenship in heaven is secured. I eagerly await Your return!

Answers

1. The curse of the Law and the curse on Adam and Eve.
2. The cultivation of the soil.
3. True, because Jesus was identified as not only the seed of Abraham but also the Son of Adam.
4. The Immanuel race, the God-man race.
5. The crown represented the curse of *thorns* and the purple robe represented the curse of *thistles*—the double curse on the earth.
6. False. It will happen at the period of "new heavens and a new earth."

24

To Bless or to Curse?

Suppose that people revile us, curse us, oppose us and persecute us for our faith in Christ. Suppose that they spread
malicious lies about us and use all sorts of dishonest and
illegal means to do us harm. Are we free to retaliate by
pronouncing some kind of curse against them? To this the
answer of the New Testament is a clear, emphatic NO!

In Romans 12:9–21 Paul lists various principles that
should govern Christian behavior. In verse 9 he begins with
the one supremely important motivation: "Let *love* be without hypocrisy" (emphasis added). All the other directions
that follow are simply different ways in which Christian
love expresses itself.

In verse 14 he instructs Christians how to respond to
those who seek to do them harm: "Bless those who persecute you; bless and do not curse."

In verse 21 he closes with a more general application
of the same principle: "Do not be overcome by evil, but
overcome evil with good." There is only one power strong
enough to overcome evil, and that is *good*. Whatever form

of evil confronts us, we must always respond with the corresponding form of good. Otherwise we shall find evil too strong for us.

In 1 Peter 3:8–9, Peter gives a similar warning against the wrong kind of reaction to evil:

> Finally, all of you be of one mind, having compassion for one another; love as brothers, be tenderhearted, be courteous; not returning evil for evil or reviling for reviling, but on the contrary blessing, knowing that you were called to this, that you may inherit a blessing.

By thus overcoming evil with good, we share in Christ's own triumph over evil, as depicted in 2 Corinthians 2:14–15:

> Now thanks be to God who always leads us in triumph in Christ, and through us diffuses the fragrance of His knowledge in every place. For we are to God the fragrance of Christ among those who are being saved and among those who are perishing.

Like Mary of Bethany, who poured costly ointment on the head of Jesus, we fill the whole area around us with a sweet fragrance. Even those who oppose us and criticize us are nevertheless blessed by the fragrance (see Mark 14:3–9).

This brings out a basic difference between the Old and the New Covenants. In the Old Testament, God frequently used His people as instruments of judgment against other people. In bringing Israel into the land of Canaan, for instance, God used Joshua and his army as the instruments of His judgment on the Canaanites who had previously occupied the land. There are also many other instances in the Old Testament in which God's servants pronounced curses on people who opposed or disobeyed Him, and the effect was the same as if God Himself had uttered them.

In Joshua 6:26, for example, after the Israelites had captured and destroyed Jericho, Joshua pronounced the following curse on anyone who would ever afterward rebuild a city on the same site: "Cursed be the man before the LORD who rises up and builds this city Jericho; he shall lay its foundation with his firstborn, and with his youngest he shall set up its gates."

About five hundred years later, during the reign of Ahab king of Israel, this curse was fulfilled, as recorded in 1 Kings 16:34.

> In his [Ahab's] days Hiel of Bethel built Jericho. He laid its foundation with Abiram his firstborn, and with his youngest son Segub he set up its gates, according to the word of the LORD, which He had spoken through Joshua the son of Nun.

In the margin of the New King James Version the phrase "with his son" is rendered "at the cost of the life of. . . ." The NASB renders it "with the loss of. . . ." The NIV renders it: "at the cost of. . . ."

This is a vivid example of the invisible forces that are continually at work in human history, and yet are so often ignored. How many secular historians today, when describing this incident, would trace the death of these two young men to words spoken by a servant of God five hundred years earlier?

It is important to notice, in 1 Kings 16:34, that the writer emphasizes that the curse was fulfilled *"according to the word of the LORD*, which He had spoken through Joshua the son of Nun" (emphasis added). Joshua was the channel through which the curse came, but the Lord was its source. This—and this alone—accounts for its effect.

David was another servant of God who pronounced curses that took effect many generations later. In Psalm 69:22–25, and again in Psalm 109:6–13, he pronounced a lengthy series of curses on some unnamed person, or persons, on account of treachery and disloyalty to a righteous man who had been unjustly accused and condemned. About one thousand years later, after the death and resurrection of Jesus, the apostles recognized that these curses of David had found their fulfillment in Judas Iscariot, who had been the betrayer of Jesus (see Acts 1:15–20).

Some of the prophets who followed David also pronounced curses that released God's judgments in various ways. In 2 Kings 1:9–12, for instance, Elijah called down fire from heaven that destroyed two successive bands of soldiers sent to arrest him. In 2 Kings 2:23–24, his successor, Elisha, cursed a group of youths who had mocked him, with the result that 42 of them were mauled by bears.

Subsequently, God used Elisha to bring miraculous healing of leprosy to the Syrian general, Naaman, who in turn offered Elisha a variety of lavish presents. Elisha, however, refused to accept any of them, thus showing Naaman that there was no way he could "pay" for his healing from God. Later, Elisha's servant, Gehazi, motivated by covetousness, ran after Naaman and, on false pretenses, persuaded Naaman to give him a substantial gift of silver and clothing (see 2 Kings 5:1–27).

When Gehazi returned, Elisha—by supernatural revelation—confronted him with his covetousness and dishonesty. Then he pronounced God's judgment on him: "'Therefore the leprosy of Naaman shall cling to you and your descendants forever.' And he went out from his presence leprous, as white as snow" (verse 27).

The effect of Elisha's curse was visible and instantaneous. Gehazi found himself afflicted by leprosy in the same advanced stage from which Naaman had just been healed. Furthermore, the same disease would continue to afflict Gehazi's descendants so long as there was one of them remaining on earth.

There is one important feature common to all the curses referred to above—whether uttered by Joshua, David, Elijah or Elisha. Each of them expressed a sovereign judgment of almighty God. *They did not proceed from the mind or will of the man who uttered them*. They were not the expression of mere human anger or vindictiveness. God sovereignly chose human channels through whom to administer His justice. There is no suggestion in Scripture that God has ever renounced His right to do this.

In the New Testament, however, God has chosen to use His servants primarily as instruments of mercy and not of judgment. The contrast between the two covenants is brought out in an incident in Luke 9:51–56. Jesus had sent messengers ahead of Him to prepare for His reception in a Samaritan village through which He intended to pass, but the Samaritans refused to receive Him. In response, James and John had asked, "Lord, do You want us to command fire to come down from heaven and consume them, just as Elijah did?" (Luke 9:54).

In reply, Jesus rebuked them for their attitude, saying: "You do not know what manner of spirit you are of. For the Son of Man did not come to destroy men's lives but to save them" (Luke 9:55–56).

Jesus did not deny that Elijah had called down fire to destroy his enemies. Nor did He question that James and John might have been able to do the same. Instead, He reminded them that they were in a period when God was using His servants in a different way. They were called to be instruments of God's mercy, rather than His judgment.

Nevertheless, there are a few instances in the New Testament of curses pronounced by God's servants. Jesus Himself provided one of the most dramatic examples. On His way into Jerusalem, becoming hungry, He went up to a fig tree to get some of the early fruit that would have been appropriate at that season. Discovering that the tree was full of leaves, but had produced no fruit, He said to it, "Let no fruit grow on you ever again" (Matthew 21:19).

Next day, when He and His disciples passed by, the fig tree had withered from the roots. Peter commented: "Rabbi,

287

look! The fig tree which You *cursed* has withered away" (Mark 11:21, emphasis added). In reply, Jesus delegated to His disciples the same authority that He Himself had demonstrated in cursing the fig tree: "Assuredly, I say to you, if you have faith and do not doubt, you will not only do what was done to the fig tree . . ." (Matthew 21:21). In other words, He gave them authority to pronounce curses similar to that which He had pronounced on the fig tree.

Many commentators see in this fig tree a type of the form of religion into which the practice of the Law of Moses had degenerated. It was full of "leaves"—but it did not yield the true fruit of the Law, which Jesus summed up as "justice and mercy and faith" (Matthew 23:23). As a result, sincere seekers who looked to that form of religion to satisfy their spiritual hunger were turned away, empty and disappointed. Within a generation, under the judgment of God, the whole system was destined to "wither from the roots."

The disciples apparently saw no significance in the fruitless fig tree, and would have passed it by. It was Jesus who took action against it, and then commissioned His disciples to take similar action. In succeeding generations, this lesson seems to have been lost on most Christians. Certainly there are times when we encounter such "fruitless fig trees"—that is, deceptive religious systems that disappoint hungry seekers after the reality of the Gospel. Do we merely pass these "fig trees" by, unconcerned? Or do we take the same kind of aggressive action that Jesus demonstrated?

In Matthew 10:14–15, when Jesus sent out the first apostles to preach the Gospel, He gave them authority of a similar kind to deal with those who rejected them and their message:

> "And whoever will not receive you nor hear your words, when you depart from that house or city, shake off the dust from your feet. Assuredly, I say to you, it will be more

tolerable for the land of Sodom and Gomorrah in the day of judgment than for that city!"

By this act of shaking off the dust from their feet, the apostles would, in effect, hand over those who rejected them to the judgment of God, which would ultimately be more severe than that on the inhabitants of Sodom and Gomorrah.

The apostles of the New Testament took this command of Jesus literally. In Pisidian Antioch, after Paul and Barnabas had ministered for some time with great effect, their adversaries finally drove them out of the city. Acts 13:51 records the apostles' response: "But they shook off the dust from their feet against them, and came to Iconium."

Incidents such as these confirm a principle already established in the Old Testament: Blessings and curses are never far separated from one another. When blessings are offered, but rejected, curses almost inevitably follow in their place. When Israel entered Canaan under the Law of Moses, God required her to invoke upon herself either the blessings promised for obedience, or the curses that followed disobedience. There was no third option. The same applies to those who have the Gospel with its blessings proclaimed to them, but deliberately and consciously reject it. Almost inevitably they expose themselves to corresponding curses.

Earlier, on the island of Cyprus, God had opened the way for Paul and Barnabas to bring the Gospel to the Roman proconsul,[1] Sergius Paulus. However, a sorcerer—that is, a practitioner of the occult—named Elymas sought to keep them from speaking to the proconsul. Paul's response to this challenge from Satan is described in Acts 13:9–12.

Then Saul, who also is called Paul, filled with the Holy Spirit, looked intently at him and said, "O full of all deceit and all fraud, you son of the devil, you enemy of all righteousness, will you not cease perverting the straight ways of the Lord? And now, indeed, the hand of the Lord is upon you, and you shall be blind, not seeing the sun for a time." And immediately a dark mist fell on him, and he went around seeking someone to lead him by the hand. Then the proconsul believed, when he saw what had been done, being astonished at the teaching of the Lord.

The effect of Paul's words on Elymas was as immediate and dramatic as the curse of leprosy that Elisha had pronounced upon Gehazi. The writer of Acts emphasizes that at this moment Paul was "filled with the Holy Spirit." Therefore, his words were not the product of his own fleshly reaction to opposition, but represented God's sovereign judgment on the sorcerer, uttered by the Holy Spirit. The proconsul was so impressed by this demonstration of the supremacy of Jesus over Satan that he became a believer.

This incident brings out the decisive issues in determining whether or not there are situations in which it is right for Christians to pronounce a curse. If the motive is some reaction of our fleshly nature, such as resentment or anger, or the desire for revenge or self-justification or self-glorification, then to utter a curse in such a situation would be a sin. Furthermore, it would do much greater harm to the one who utters the curse than to the one who is cursed.

In Romans 6:16 Paul emphasizes the danger of yielding to this kind of satanic motivation:

Don't you know that when you offer yourselves to someone to obey him as slaves, you are slaves to the one whom you obey—whether you are slaves to sin, which leads to death, or to obedience, which leads to righteousness?

NIV

It can be tempting to seek momentary gratification of some evil impulse by allowing a curse to pass through our lips, but in so doing we offer ourselves as slaves to the author of the temptation: Satan. He is not content with merely temporary influence over us. He uses the temptation as an opening through which he can move in and take permanent control of our lives. Our temporary yielding to him thus becomes permanent enslavement. In this way, *the one who uses a curse to bring evil upon others brings a far greater and more enduring evil upon himself.*

On the other hand, the New Testament gives clear examples of situations in which the Holy Spirit sovereignly chose to pronounce a curse through a servant of God. If we refuse to acknowledge this possibility, we shut ourselves off from one of the ways in which God might wish to use us. Our only safeguard is to cultivate a relationship with the Holy Spirit in which we are sensitive both to His prompting and to His restraining. If we have any doubts as to the purity of our motives or the leading of the Holy Spirit, we should most certainly keep silent.

The possibility that the Holy Spirit may in certain circumstances prompt us to utter a curse was made very real to me by an incident that occurred in my ministry in the mid-1960s. At that time I was part of the ministerial staff of a church located in the inner city of Chicago. The building immediately adjoining the church was a pub. This had become a center for various forms of vice, which included drug-peddling, knife fights and prostitution—both male and female.

One evening I was on the platform of the church, leading a meeting of people gathered to pray for the city of Chicago. In the midst of the prayer, without any premeditation on my part, I heard myself make a loud declaration: "I put the curse of the Lord on that pub!" After that, the meeting continued along its normal course. Personally, I gave little further thought to what I had said.

About two months later, I was awakened at 3 A.M. by an urgent phone call to say that the church was on fire. I dressed and hurried to the scene, to discover that it was not the church, but the pub next door, that was on fire. The wind off Lake Michigan, however, was blowing the flames onto the church. Just when it seemed inevitable that the church would be destroyed along with the pub, the direction of the wind suddenly changed 180 degrees and blew the flames away from the church.

In the end, the pub was completely destroyed and the church suffered only smoke damage, which was fully covered by insurance. No lives were lost, and no one was injured. After surveying the scene and what had taken place, the fire chief commented to the senior elder of the church: "You people must have a special relationship with the Man upstairs!"

My personal reaction was one of awe, mingled with fear. I had no doubt that what I had witnessed was the outworking of the curse on the pub that I had pronounced two months earlier. I did not regret what I had done. I felt that God had intervened in righteous judgment, tempered with mercy. At the same time, I realized in a new way the awesome power that could be released through words spoken by a servant of God. I resolved that, for my part, I would seek God for His grace never to misuse that power.

On a small scale, the destruction of that pub by fire reinforces a truth of Scripture that is central to this whole theme of blessings and curses: *The power of the tongue is measureless—whether for good or for evil*. With our tongue we can bless and we can curse; we can build up and we can break down; we can wound and we can heal; we can do great good, and just as great harm.

The power of the tongue is also frightening, because we ourselves cannot control it. Again and again, our experience compels us to acknowledge the truth of James 3:8: "But no man can tame the tongue." There is therefore only one safe course: to yield the tongue to God through the Holy Spirit and ask Him to control it for us. To help us do this, here are two prayers of David that are patterns for us to follow:

Set a guard, O Lord, over my mouth; keep watch over the door of my lips.

Psalm 141:3

Let the words of my mouth and the meditation of my heart be acceptable in Your sight, O Lord, my strength and my Redeemer.

Psalm 19:14

Questions for the Study —————————————

1. According to Romans 12:14, how should we re- *bless*
   spond to those who are trying to persecute us? *them*
2. What is the one power strong enough to overcome
   evil? *good*
3. In the New Testament God has called His people
   to be instruments of His *mercy* and not of His
   judgment
4. True or false: Blessings and curses are never far
   separated from one another. *T*
5. The one who uses a curse to bring evil on others
   brings a far *greater* and more *enduring* evil on
   himself.
6. According to Psalm 141:3, what should we do to
   help control the use of our tongue? *ask God to
   set a guard over our mouth*

Life Application —————————————

1. How do you think blessing the person who is cursing you affects him or her, and what does it accomplish in your life?
2. How can you be an instrument of mercy?
3. Do you now have a better understanding of the
   power of the tongue? In what way?

Memory Verse —————————————

Bless those who persecute you; bless and do not
curse.

Romans 12:14

Faith Response —————————————

*Lord, I choose to be an instrument of mercy by blessing, en-
couraging and demonstrating love to those around me.*

Answers

1. Bless them and do not curse them.
2. The power of good.
3. Mercy, judgment.
4. True. If blessings are rejected, curses inevitably follow in their place.
5. Greater, enduring.
6. Ask the Lord to set a guard over our mouths.

Notes

Chapter 2
1. See Revelation 12:1–12.

Chapter 5
1. The numbers in parentheses indicate verses in Deuteronomy 28 that speak of similar conditions. In some cases, the words used in the New International Version are included beside those of the New King James Version.

Chapter 6
1. It is significant that the word *fascination* is derived from a Latin verb that means "to bewitch."

2. A drachma was about a day's wage. At today's rates in the United States, the total amount could easily be $2,000,000.

Chapter 7
1. Joshua 8:32–35 records how this ceremony was actually carried out after Israel had entered the land of Canaan.

Chapter 8
1. This second verb here translated "to curse" also means "to revile," "to speak evil of."

Chapter 9
1. See Ephesians 1:22.

Chapter 11
1. *Webster's Dictionary* defines *anarchy* as: 1. The complete absence of government. 2. political disorder and violence; lawlessness. 3. disorder in any sphere of activity.

2. They were first hanged, then their corpses were dragged through the street by a horse or some other animal, and finally cut up into four pieces.

Chapter 12
1. Anyone interested in a comprehensive study of this subject is referred to the book *Freemasonry: An Interpretation* by Martin L. Wagner (obtainable from HRT Ministries, Box 12, Newtonville, N.Y. 12128-0012).

Chapter 13
1. Quoted from *America: The Sorcerer's New Apprentice* by Dave Hunt and T. A. McMahon (Eugene, Ore.: Harvest House Publishers, 1988).

Chapter 17
1. Other implications of this verse were discussed in chapter 5 on page 61.

Chapter 18
1. See Matthew 9:21–22; 14:36; Mark 5:23, 28, 34; 6:56; 10:52; Luke 8:48; Acts 4:9; 14:9; James 5:15.

2. See Luke 8:36.

3. See Luke 8:50.

4. See John 11:12.

Chapter 22
1. This is dealt with more fully in chapter 24.

Chapter 24
1. A senior Roman official.

Index

298

Index

Index

Derek Prince (1915–2003) was born in India of British parents. He was educated as a scholar of Greek and Latin at Eton College and Cambridge University, England, where he held a fellowship in ancient and modern philosophy at King's College. He also studied several modern languages, including Hebrew and Aramaic, at Cambridge University and the Hebrew University in Jerusalem.

While serving with the British army in World War II, Derek began to study the Bible and experienced a life-changing encounter with Jesus Christ. Out of that encounter he formed two conclusions: first, that Jesus Christ is alive; and second, that the Bible is a true, relevant, up-to-date book. These conclusions altered the whole course of his life, which he then devoted to studying and teaching the Bible.

Derek's main gift of explaining the Bible and its teaching in a clear, simple way has helped build a foundation of faith in millions of lives. His nondenominational, nonsectarian approach makes his teaching relevant and helpful to people from all racial and religious backgrounds.

He wrote more than fifty books, and his teaching is featured on five hundred audio and 160 video teaching cassettes, many of which have been translated and published in more than sixty languages. His daily radio broadcast, *Derek Prince Legacy Radio*, is translated into Arabic, Chinese (Amoy, Cantonese, Mandarin, Shanghaiese, Swatow), Croatian, German, Malagasy, Mongolian, Russian, Samoan, Spanish, and Tongan. His daily radio program continues to touch lives around the world.

For more information on Derek Prince and the many teaching resources available, please contact:

Derek Prince Ministries
P.O. Box 19501
Charlotte, NC 28219-9501
(704) 357-3556
www.derekprince.org